HOW TO GET SUPER RICH IN THE OPPORTUNITY MARKET! 2

BY T.J. ROHLEDER

TABLE OF CONTENTS:

Let Me Make You Rich!

How I Have Made Millions in the Lucrative Business Opportunity Market... and So Can You.

What you are about to discover is a little-known home-based business that can make you very rich! You can get started for <u>less</u> than a few thousand dollars (we started with $300.00 back in 1988) — and it is very possible to turn this small sum into many thousands of dollars a month in a very short period of time!

Not to brag, but my wife Eileen and I (along with the help we received from marketing expert Russ von Hoelscher) turned our $300.00 investment into a grand total of over $10,000,000.00 in our first 5 years. And that was just the beginning. Since then we have been on a mission to learn all of the secrets I'm about to share with you in this book to generate over $150,000,000.00 in our first 24 years alone.

And Now I Will Do My Best to Help You Get Rich in This Lucrative Marketplace.

Here are a Dozen Reasons Why this booming market can let you stay home and potentially make more money than you doctor or lawyer is earning right now...

1. **Millions of people want to give you their money.** These people continue to buy and re-buy all kinds of business opportunities. They are spending a fortune. **All you have to do is know what to offer them and they'll gladly give their money to you!**

2. **You can make awesome profits for the rest of your life.** It's fairly easy to bring in a million dollars a year in this market. And there are plenty of opportunities for you to generate even more than that. Just follow our example (along with our personal help, support and guidance which at the time I am writing this is also available to you) and you could get super rich!

3. **This market is recession proof!** In fact, we have made even more money when the economy suffers (while always providing extreme value to our customers, of course).

4. **Even idiots are making millions of dollars.** Most people are shocked when they see the kind of worthless garbage being sold by some people in the opportunity market. As you'll see; many people are getting rich selling all kinds of trash.

    You'll be shocked when you discover the simple and easy secrets our company is using to rise way above the competition and become one of the elite companies in this market. (HINT: It's not that hard when you know the secret.)

5. **The money keeps flowing in year after year!** This GIANT market keeps replenishing itself very quickly. What does that mean? TONS OF NEW BUYERS! In fact, there are millions of hungry new buyers each year who are actively searching for a proven way to make money.

6. **Developing your own business opportunity is super easy.** Over the years we have reduced this down to a system that works like a well-oiled machine! We've made millions of dollars by developing and promoting one business opportunity after another. It's so simple and easy. At one time we were marketing a new business opportunity every month. **And some of them generated millions of dollars.** I'll show you how you can do it too!

7. **There is no real competition.** This market is so BIG and so hungry that competition has never been a problem. In fact, one of our greatest secrets is how we have made millions of dollars by working closely with some of our smartest competitors.

8. **It's easy to make a lot of money in the opportunity market!** That's why this market has always attracted so many fly-by-nighters... It seems like the most dishonest people are always attracted to the lure of easy money. **But there are plenty of good honest people in this marketplace — AND WE NEED MORE!**

Listen, there's nothing wrong with making super

easy money as long as you're providing real value and <u>not</u> cheating people. Sure, there are some folks in this market who rip people off. Every market has this element. **But there is a tremendous potential for any honest person to become a multi-millionaire in this market.**

9.   **There are many proven, time-tested shortcuts to getting rich in this market.** The path has already been laid by people like Joe Karbo, Russ von Hoelscher, David Bendah, Harvey Brody, and others. These people were the pioneers who paved the way for companies like ours. Many proven "models" exist for this lucrative business. **This book (and the FIRST "How to Get Super Rich in the Opportunity Market" book I authored) gives you top methods that have brought us millions of dollars.** Just pick one or two of these methods and you could make a lot of money, just like we have. Find a way to use all of the methods and strategies we have to teach and you could potentially make a lot more money than we're making!

10.   **Making money in the opportunity market is the most RISK-FREE wealth-maker ever.** Millions of prospective buyers in the opportunity market are obsessed with finding the greatest ways to make more money. It's all they think about. **We make our money by creating easy-to-assemble 'turn-key systems' for these people to profit by promoting various products and services that we discover or develop for them.** The customers we sell to keep buying again and

again! In fact, some of our customers have been giving us thousands of dollars, year after year. And you now have some of our greatest secrets! **As you'll see, I have done my best to reduce everything down to a simple formula that makes it <u>almost</u> impossible to lose money.**

11. **You can get rich fast!** We started in September of 1988 with only $300.00 and quickly turned it into a grand total of over $10,000.00 in our first five years. **Since that time we've tried lots of different things that you'll read about in this book (and the first "How to Get Super Rich in the Opportunity Market" book I authored). We have honed our best ideas into specific formulas and strategies that make money... like magic!** Just follow our recipe for making millions of dollars that I will freely share with you in both of my books (and many other books and audio programs I have produced over the years) and <u>you</u> could potentially make millions, too. Best of all, the money can come to you super fast!

12. **The more competitors there are in this market, the more money we all can make.** This marketplace is insatiable! There are millions of hungry prospects to buy from you and me. **Most of my competitors in this marketplace do not understand how lucrative it is!** These people are happy to plod along to make $50,000.00 $100,000.00 a year. That's okay for them, and you may be happy with making this amount of money. But if you want to get super rich, I can show you

how to do that, too!

Why Give You These Secrets?

Well first, this lucrative marketplace is huge and growing. Because of this, there's plenty of room for thousands of other companies like ours. There's room for you, too, if you want to take a shot at the millions of dollars that are waiting to be made!

Second, this marketplace needs more honest people who sincerely want to help people make money and fulfill their dreams. The more honest people who are serving this marketplace, the better.

And third, I'm constantly on the lookout for people I can joint venture with. And who is better to work with than someone that I have helped to train? NO ONE!

Listen: Some of the best times and most fulfilling moments I've had in the opportunity market is when I was collaborating and doing various joint venture business deals with a group of my competitors who I also consider my friends. I sincerely hope that you will get excited about this business and become someone I can work with on a regular basis. You'll find my personal contact information (and an AMAZING FREE BONUS GIFT!) at the end of this Introduction. Please contact me and lets strive to become joint venture business partners and friends...

But before I digress further... Let's get back to what makes the opportunity market such a powerful way to make money.

ADVANTAGE #1 - Millions of hungry buyers are happily spending huge sums of their money on all kinds of opportunities.

This marketplace is loaded with RABID BUYERS.

Millions of people are obsessed with making more money. **These people are spending a large portion of their disposable income on a wide variety of plans and programs that offer to show them how to make a fortune.**

Business opportunities are a multi-billion dollar market. This market is full of people who sell everything from $14.95 books, to $500.00 plans, to $500,000.00 franchises. *All of the buyers have one thing in common:* They're obsessed with finding the best way to make the most money. Once an obsession takes over, there's no stopping it!

Why do the millions of people in the opportunity market spend so much of their money on all these plans and programs?

That's simple:

The Desire to Make Money is the Most Powerful Motivating Force on Earth.

We live in a society that worships money. This is a powerful force that can rule peoples' lives from the cradle to the grave. And having more money can help solve many of life's biggest challenges.

With enough money, we can live the lives we dream of. We can have the best of everything. Money is freedom! **It's the freedom to live the way you want and do what you want.** While others struggle to pay their bills, you can be relaxing on the beach or hanging out at Starbucks drinking a $5 cup of coffee and reading a great book and not feeling guilty about it.

Have a favorite cause or organization you'd love to support? Money gives you the freedom to donate often and in huge amounts.

It's all about having choices. And let's face it, whatever your idea of the good life is, it usually takes a certain amount of money to afford it.

And that's great news for those of us in the opportunity market. Because we are in the business of helping people make more money.

Many people who buy business opportunities send away for plan after plan in an attempt to find the perfect one that will turn everything around for them.

These people are frustrated. They are hungry for success. It's an obsession! And they spend huge sums of money in an attempt to satisfy their obsession. These people buy and re-buy. **You just have to know what to offer them and at they'll buy from you!**

ADVANTAGE #2 — This market can make you GIANT sums of money for the rest of your life!

Millions of people want to make more money, and all you need are a very small percentage of them to buy and re-buy from you. This is very easy to do in the opportunity market, because once people trust you they'll keep doing business with you.

We have customers who have been buying from us for over 10 years. And some of these people have spent tens of thousands of dollars. They keep coming back and spending more money on the products and services we develop for them. They're insatiable. And they love the programs we sell and they keep coming back to buy everything new that we offer them.

Now listen carefully...

Millions of people keep buying money-making opportunities year after year. And millions of <u>new prospects</u> are getting bitten by the money-making bug every year!

It's an itch they have to scratch... Most people say they want to make more money, but for many of these people, the desire to scratch that itch goes away... For one reason or another — fear, negative influences, whatever — they resist the urge to scratch. **But not so for the all of the prospective buyers in the opportunity market! These people become obsessed with finding a way to make a lot of money.**

It starts when they answer an ad in the back of a magazine or get excited about an infomercial that promises a better life. They buy one time, in an attempt to improve their life. **And that small purchase leads to more. It fans the flames of their desire!** The more of these business and money-making opportunities they buy, the more they want to buy...

The very act of making that very first purchase
— scratching that itch for the first time —
is like pouring a 55 gallon drum of gasoline on a fire.

Each purchase makes them even <u>more</u> interested in making money...

Soon their name is sold to other companies who promote business opportunities... Now 'Joe Prospect' goes to his mailbox every day to find it stuffed with all kinds of offers from other people who sell money-making programs. **<u>The more he buys, the more mailing lists he ends up on</u>.** Everyone in the opportunity market claims to have the ultimate plan or system for making money, *and soon Joe is sending away for every program that sounds unique...* Scratching away at that itch...

All you have to do is know how to quickly find, develop and promote the very <u>best</u> money-making opportunities that this huge market of people want to buy, and they will stand in line with money in hand and practically beg you to take it!

This market is hungry and huge.

Think of the opportunity market as if it were a giant bank vault that's filled with hundreds of millions of dollars. All you have to do is know the combination to the safe and you can get rich!

<u>Here's the formula</u>:

- There are millions of hungry buyers for the products and services we sell.

- It's simple and even easy to develop business opportunity programs and turn-key systems that have the potential to help these people make money.

- You can do business with these people again and again for maximum profits!

These millions of opportunity buyers have an insatiable appetite and they buy from many different companies. In fact, **the same people who give our company thousands of dollars can give <u>you</u> thousands of dollars, too.**

And remember, this is a market that could potentially make you even more money in bad economic times. *That leads us to the next major advantage...*

ADVANTAGE #3 — You make money in good times or bad! In fact, a slump or downturn in the economy could make you even more money.

Many businesses only do well when the economy is good. People only buy those products and services when they are not worried about the future...

Not so with the opportunity market. This is a market that does great in good times and can do even better in bad times!

In fact...

A down-swing in the economy can be an up-swing for you!

Now granted, no one wants to see the economy go into the dumps—and a total market crash would not be good for anybody, but a recession in the economy can be good for those of us who sell business opportunities. It jolts people out of their sleep. As they become a little nervous about the economy, the pain of uncertainty causes them to seek out ways to get in business for themselves!

We have gone through several periods of recession where all of the other businesses we knew of were suffering... *while our profits soared!*

Of course, this business also does great in times of prosperity. People are feeling good about life, there's a positive spirit in the air, and everyone is spending more money. They feel more at ease to spend some of their money on business opportunities.

Now here's the exciting part...

The more you understand about this market, and the shortcut secrets to making more money, the <u>less</u> you will worry about the economy.

You can continue to make more and more money, no

matter what happens to the economy, no matter which political party is in office, and no matter what's happening on Wall Street. Sure, some months will be better than others. But your business will be much less prone to suffer through the ups and downs that most businesses go through.

You'll have the ability that few people have:

The ability to make money at will!

Your sales and profits can grow as high as you want! The sky is the limit. And that takes us to the next powerful advantage of this world's greatest business...

ADVANTAGE #4 — This market has the awesome power to make you a millionaire in no time flat!

As I've said, this is a HUGE market of millions of hungry prospects with money to spend. These are rabid buyers! They are hungry for all the things that the right business can give them. These people will gladly give you huge sums of money if you can help them get what they want.

All you have to know is what to sell them and they'll beat a path to your door with money in hand!

Think of the opportunity market as a giant safe that's filled with tens of millions of dollars! Just know the magic numbers to unlock this safe and all the money inside can be yours.

This is a market that can truly make you richer than your wildest dreams. It has generated a fortune for me and many other people... And it can produce a mega-fortune for you, too!

This is, of course, no promise that you will become a millionaire in this market, or make any specific sum of money. All businesses have risks. But I firmly believe that once you have our greatest secrets that are in BOTH of my "How to Get Super Rich in the Opportunity Market" books (and in many of my other books and audio programs) and use these secrets like we do, you can make more money than you've ever dreamed you could make.

ADVANTAGE #5 — The opportunity market is the world's largest niche market.

The first secret to major riches is a deep understanding of the exact type of person who is most likely to buy from you. **The more you know about this person, the more money you can make!**

A niche market is simply a group of prospects or customers who have enough in common that to know one of them is to know all of them...

This gives you the power to develop products and services you <u>know</u> these people really want. You know them like you know all your best friends. You understand what excites them the most... **And this gives you the awesome power to make <u>THE</u> <u>MAXIMUM</u> amount of money by only selling them what they want the most.**

People who sell to niche markets are able to make money where others fail because:

✔   They know <u>exactly</u> what these people want to buy.

✔   They know how to speak to these people <u>the right way</u> to get their full attention and interest.

✔   And they know how to easily convince these people that what you're offering them is way more valuable than the money in their pocket!

This knowledge gives them incredible money-making power. Now they can reach the niche market with the <u>right</u> kind of message that will break through THE THICK CLUTTER of all the other advertising messages. Their understanding of the exact type of people who are most likely to give them their money is their power to get super rich.

As a niche marketer, you can build a group of people who will continue to buy from you year after year. Plus, you'll have a proven way to get all the new customers you want. The bigger the niche market, the more money you can make!

PROBLEM: Most niche markets are very small. Sure, the companies in these markets are making HUGE profits, but there's only so much money to be made in these small markets...

SOLUTION: The opportunity market is HUGE! This market is made up of many tens of millions of hungry prospects. <u>And all of these people have a great deal in common</u>.

That's why I call this...

The World's Biggest Niche Market!

To know one Customer in the opportunity market is to know millions of them. This means your ad or sales letter or words on your website can be seen by millions of people who share the same powerful interest: the desire to get rich. Now all you have to know is <u>what</u> to say and <u>how</u> to say it, and a generous percentage of these people will gladly give you their money! **You will have the combination to the secret safe that's crammed full of <u>millions</u> of dollars.** Just a few clicks on the dial and this money can be yours!

There are certain things that almost everyone in the

opportunity market really wants. Just know what these things are and how to give it to them, and you could make more money than all the richest doctors and lawyers in your area!

But that's not all! There's more! You see, there's ONE MORE POWERFUL ADVANTAGE you must know about that has the potential power to make you super rich...

ADVANTAGE #6 — Creating Super Hot Million Dollar Products and Services Is About As Much Fun As You Can Have With Your Clothes On!

Sales material and product development are the most fulfilling parts of this business! It is so exciting and rewarding to come up with an idea for a product or service that produces millions of dollars. And the better you get at this, the easier it is! Creating multi-million dollar products and services for this marketplace is the ultimate money-making game. You start with the seed of your idea, watch it grow, scatter it out into the market, and watch the millions of dollars flow back to you!

There is nothing more exciting than watching an idea you came up with produce millions of dollars. It feels so great you just want to keep doing it! This is addictive!

I have a sign in my office that says, "Happiness Is A Positive Cash Flow!" And it's true. **Once you experience the thrill of millions of dollars pouring in, you'll be hooked for life!**

That's what happened to me. YOU CAN BE NEXT. *Read on as I show you...*

How We Turned $300 into Over $10-MILLION in Our First 5 Years with These Amazing Secrets!

My wife, Eileen, and I got started in the opportunity

market back in September of 1988 with only $300.00 and a really great idea for a red-hot money-making plan. We wrote a simple booklet about our plan, and ran a tiny ad in a national magazine to sell it.

We ran the small ad with $300.00 we got from selling a beat-up 1983 Chevy Van and became millionaires in less than 5 years. The rest, shall we say, is history.

The money flowed in faster than we could spend it. We were shocked and stunned! We walked around like zombies for the first year or two. We were living in a daze!

>> We could not believe this was FINALLY happening to us! <<

Here we were, two 'kids' in our late 20s who had <u>never</u> made more than $28,000.00 in a single year. And now millions of dollars was pouring into our small farmhouse a mile outside of Goessel, Kansas. It was almost unbelievable. Each day more and more money came flowing in than we even knew what to do with!

We kept pinching each other just to make sure we weren't dreaming!

We spent the first few years like two kids in a candy story. This was the most thrilling experience in our lives! In less than 5 years, we had taken our tiny $300 ad and turned it into a grand total of ten-million dollars! This was an amazing roller coaster ride for us. Our entire lives were changed forever!

We had stumbled onto a way to wealth that was so simple a child could do it. <u>We were absolutely shocked and amazed at how simple and easy it was to get rich in the opportunity market</u>! And this has amazed us ever since.

I have been in the opportunity market ever since. That

was many years ago and on many days I'm <u>still</u> like a little kid in the candy store. Every day huge stacks of orders come pouring into our office in little Goessel, Kansas. We get orders by phone, fax, and email 24 hours a day, 7 days a week — even when we're not in the office. **It takes my staff several hours each day just to sort out all these orders, process all the credit cards, and see that our Clients get <u>MORE</u> than they paid for.** (Yes, I have a staff of hardworking people who work for me full time — and others who work for me part-time. But that's completely optional. I'll show you how to have money pouring in even if you want nothing to do with hiring employees or having an office outside of your home.)

I'm not telling you any of this to brag. **All I'm trying to do is tell you my story, so you can get a good idea of what's possible for you.** Just follow the same methods and strategies we use and you could have a business that brings you millions of dollars too!

In both of my "How to Get Super Rich in the Opportunity Market" books (and other books and audio programs I'll gladly send you), I will walk you through some of our ultimate secrets for making a large fortune in the smallest period of time. **<u>THERE'S A LOT TO LEARN, BUT NOTHING WILL EVER BE HELD BACK FROM YOU</u>.** You'll be shocked and amazed when you discover just how simple and easy it can be to make a huge fortune!

Getting millions of dollars in this market is easier than you can imagine... I'm living-proof that it can be done.

So read this book closely. Nothing will be held back from you. Each chapter gives you one multi-million dollar secret after another. You will discover some of the greatest shortcut secrets we use to make our fortune. These are secrets and methods and strategies that took many years of sweat, blood, and tears to discover.

There is nothing special about me. I'm just an ambitious guy who was lucky enough to stumble onto an amazingly lucrative business that very few people fully understand. The few people who truly do have a deep understanding of this market are making a fortune. Some of these people will hate me for sharing my greatest million dollar secrets with you, but who cares? Many of them do not realize just how enormous and lucrative this market is... They are ignorant to think that there will be less money for them if more people like you start making huge sums of money.

That is pure, unadulterated horse manure!

Bringing more honest and ethical people into this market is great for <u>all</u> of us. This lucrative market is on the move. Thanks to the Internet and other new high-tech innovations, this market will only continue to grow and prosper.

And as it grows, you can be one of the lucky few who were smart enough to get into this lucrative market. So please read this book very carefully. And do order my first "How to Get Super Rich in the Opportunity Market!" book. It's available at Amazon.com and contains our rare and unusual A-to-Z Wealth-Making Formula that has the power to make you all the money you want, need and truly deserve!

And to reward you for purchasing this book, I have...

A great FREE business-building gift for you!

Yes, I have a gift waiting for you that can DRAMATICALLY INCREASE YOUR SALES AND PROFITS!

Here's what it's all about: I spent TEN FULL YEARS writing down all of the greatest marketing and success secrets I discovered during that time period. Each day, I took a few notes, and at the end of a decade, I had a GIANT LIST of 6,159 powerful secrets! This list is ALMOST 1,000 PAGES of hardcore money-making ideas and strategies!**

Best of all, this massive collection is now YOURS ABSOLUTELY FREE! Just go to: www.6159FreeSecrets.com and get it NOW! As you'll see; this complete collection of 6,159 of my greatest marketing and success secrets, far more valuable than those you can buy from others for $495.00 to $997.00, is yours absolutely **FREE**, with no cost, no obligation.

Why am I giving away this GIANT COLLECTION of secrets that took ONE DECADE to discover and compile FOR FREE? That's simple, I believe many of the people who receive these 6,159 secrets in this huge 955 page PDF document will want to obtain some of my other books and audio programs and participate in our special COACHING PROGRAMS. However, you are NOT obligated to buy anything — now or ever.

I know you're serious about making more money or you wouldn't be reading this. So go to: www.6159FreeSecrets.com and get this complete collection of 6,159 of my greatest marketing and success secrets right now! **You'll get this GREAT FREE GIFT in the next few minutes, just for letting me add you to my Client mailing list,** and I'll stay in touch with you... and do all I can to help you make even more money with my proven marketing strategies and methods.

So with all this said, let's begin...

** **WARNING:** This complete collection of 6,159 marketing and success secrets (that you can receive right now... for no cost!) contains MANY CONTROVERSIAL ideas and methods. Also, it was originally written for MY EYES ONLY and for a few VERY CLOSE FRIENDS. Therefore, the language is X-RATED in some places (I got VERY EXCITED when I wrote many of these ideas and used VERY FOUL LANGUAGE to get my ideas across!) so 'IF' you are EASILY OFFENDED or do NOT want to read anything OFFENSIVE, then please do both of us a favor and DO NOT go to my website and download this FREE gift. THANK YOU for your understanding.

1

Master the Skills of Information Marketing

The secret that we used to make millions of dollars is this: We honed our skills in product development. **My entire life changed the day I created our first information product,** *Dialing for Dollars.* I look at it now, and it looks like some kind of a joke. It was poorly written, filled with typos; it just wasn't a good program in any way. Yet that was product that got us started, and it was just a little booklet that we sold for $12.95. We ran a small ad in an opportunity magazine, using the last $300 we had.

But the program clicked with our prospects, because it was based on something that we had been using that was totally proven. That was the only great thing about *Dialing for Dollars,* and yet it got us started and the customers loved it. Then I started writing *Dialing for Dollars, Part II* just a few months later, and I started putting my heart and soul into a better program. The first one included some multilevel marketing aspects, and I just didn't like that; it was creating too many problems, and my wife was begging me to stop doing it. She wanted me to take all the multilevel marketing stuff out. So I started working on *Dialing for Dollars Part II,* which became our new and expanded *Dialing for Dollars* program, and with that program the multilevel stuff; it just went out of the window. **It became a straight distributorship opportunity — and people loved the idea of making money with an answering machine.** It resonated; people were absolutely crazy about it. This was in the late-1980s, when answering machines were brand new and technology was making them more affordable, even as they were shrinking in size and increasing in power — and people loved the idea that there was a way to make money with this new technology.

Ever since then we've continued to use that theme, as when we showed people how to make money with computer bulletin boards. When the Internet came around, we showed people how to make money with websites. People love the idea of new technology. They're just crazy over it, and they're always looking for some way to make money with new technology. It's exciting to them, it's interesting, and we really did *start* with our last $300. This was all the money we had at the time. We sold a beat-up van we'd used for our carpet-cleaning business to get that little bit of money, which gave us an opportunity to buy a tiny ad in one of the best moneymaking magazines of the time. **Now, the first *Dialing for Dollars* was a glorified brochure!** That's all it was. **It wasn't anything that we would produce today, and yet the customers liked it, and it really worked for them.** It really made them money. That was especially true after we came up with *Dialing for Dollars, Part II.* We got away from the multilevel marketing aspect. We showed people how to use their answering machine to sell the products we'd created, although we also showed them how they could use it for other things besides just our products. **They found our honesty and**

integrity refreshing.

Once we came up with the idea of tiny manuals that were designed to sell in newspapers, **we took a couple of different opportunities that were working for us and blended them together to create this whole** *Dialing for Dollars* **concept.** The ideas are out there, folks; and **we happened to hit on the right ideas at the right time.** Little did we know it, but our idea resonated and it actually made people money, and that's a great thing. To be able to really, truly help people make money is wonderful.

> **L**ife, love, and business favor the BOLD!

We had distributors who were making $10,000, $20,000, $50,000 a month. We had one guy in Utah who was making $5 million a year before he cut us out (as all of our successful distributors ultimately do), and that was back when our company was barely doing a couple of million dollars a year. So we had a distributor who was doing more than twice as well as us, and that's a great thing! It makes me really happy that we helped people. **That's one of the things that a good information product can do: It can really make a difference in people's lives. This was the foundation of our success.**

Within six months from the time we ran that $300 ad, we were bringing in $16,000 a month, and the strategy we used was very simple. It's one that you could use starting tomorrow. We ran that little ad; it did take about six weeks before it came out, but we used those six weeks as a way of gearing up and getting things ready to go. During the six weeks we were waiting for that ad to run, we were frantically creating that little booklet. The kind of product development that took me a month to do back then I can do in a couple of days now. That's not to brag; the fact is that you get better as you go along. I want you to think about that; you've got to get started, you've got to bloom where you're planted. So get started.

Within six months we were averaging $16,000 dollars a month, and Eileen and I were like two kids in a candy store. That was more money than we'd ever made in our whole lives. We didn't even know what to *do* with that money. **Then we met Russ von Hoelscher, and Russ helped us go from $16,000 a month to almost $100,000 a week within the first nine months.** One of the things he did was help polish our product-development skills.

Our first product with Russ von Hoelscher was called *The $2,500 Weekend*, **and for us it was a major breakthrough.** That was the first time we did over $1 million on just one product, and we did it *fast*. **Now, that product took one weekend of our lives to create, but we're still using it. The sales letter took me three months to write, but we're still using parts of that sales letter** *right now*. People loved the idea of *The $2,500 Weekend*. It was such a simple idea, just like *Dialing for Dollars* was a simple idea, but it resonated in the minds and hearts of the people who bought it. Here's where we got the name: We were paying Russ von Hoelscher $2,500 every single time he came down to spend a weekend with us, and the whole time he was there, we were working on ideas and brainstorming. He was sharing his greatest tips, tricks and strategies with us, and so I said, "Russ, why don't you come down here next time, and we'll a have a recorder set up. Let's ask you a million and one questions and get all your answers — ask you all kinds of questions that we know our customers have about mail order and making money, getting rich, and that type of thing. We'll go ahead and pay you your $2,500 plus your airfare, and then we'll be very honest and direct with the customers and let them know this is material that cost us $2,500." **We sold the product at $295 — so our customers were getting $2,500 in real value for a little over a tenth of that price. This product was real and it was raw; it was honest.** All we did was put a little tape player on our kitchen table. It was all unedited, unpolished, and genuine — and that's exactly what people want. They don't want anything fancy. The more you can create informational products that are just for them, products that are perceived as having been created just for them, the better.

You don't have to be professional; you don't have to be polished. In fact, it's better that you aren't. As you may or may not be aware, this book was adapted from an audio product, part of which I recorded in my basement studio. During that recording, I tried to express myself fully, honestly. I was surrounded with notes; I didn't just make all this up on a whim. I put a lot of concentrated thought into it, but at the same time, the original recording (and this book, too) is just me trying to reach out to you, trying to help you understand the secrets that made *us* millions of dollars so they can make *you* millions of dollars. When I'm producing an audio program or hosting a seminar, I'm not trying to be a professional speaker; I'm just trying to be me. **And that's what people really want; they don't want you to play games with them.** People want information that's going to help them. The *$2,500 Weekend* made us more than a million bucks because it was targeted; **it was designed to help our customers get the information that they wanted and needed.** It touched them emotionally, and they identified with us.

We gave people what they really wanted, and they rewarded us with very quickly with well over $1 million. **It was a wonderful experience for us to realize that we could go down**

to a Radio Shack, buy a $50 cassette tape recorder, and record a product that brought us in a fortune. These days, I record on a computer, using equipment that cost thousands of dollars. Back then, I was using equipment that cost $50, and

> The best ideas are always an expansion and combination of previous ideas that worked.

there was no real difference. The product was valuable in the minds and hearts of the customers who bought it. **It resonated with them; it gave them what they wanted; it gave them what they needed.** They loved it. **I want to stress the importance of this to you, and how simple and easy it is for you to develop your own informational products.** You do have to think things through very carefully; you have to think about your customers. **There are specific things you need to do, and yet it's very easy as long as your heart is in the right place — as long as you really do want to help people.** Information products are an extension of you. They're a way for you to reach out to other people and try to make a difference in their lives, and try to share a part of who you are with them, and try to extend your hand and pull them up. In the process you pull yourself up; you make a lot of money. **The profit margins are incredible on these types of products, which really do give people what they want.**

In the opportunity market there are two basic types of products. **There are what we call soft products and hard products.** A soft product is just like this one: It gives your customers great ideas and shortcut secrets, proven strategies; it gives them personal stories from your own life that will help teach them the things that you want them to learn. It's an extension of you, and it lets you reach out and help people. **A hard product is a product like our** *Dialing for Dollars*. **It gives customers**

something to sell, either a product or a service or some combination of both. It contains, NUMBER ONE, something to sell. NUMBER TWO, it contains the sales material that you've developed for them that they can use to sell the product or service. NUMBER THREE, it contains the marketing system you developed and put together for them, so they can use that sales material to go out and promote this product or service and sell it. It's some kind of a distributorship manual that puts it all together in one cohesive package. **That's it! Just those three things.**

Hard products are what sell the most in our marketplace. The fastest way to become a millionaire in the opportunity market is to develop hard products and turn-key distributorships. We have some of them, right now, which we make available for you to sell in this marketplace. **That's what people really want: hard, turn-key products that let them go out and make money right away.** All this gets easier as you go along, and your confidence and knowledge will develop. It's all about serving your customers.

Here are ten things that all great information products have in common. NUMBER ONE: they speak to the person who buys them, just like I'm trying to speak to you right now; they're real, just like I told you about our *$2,500 Weekend* program. That program was real, and it was raw. Products like this give people something they really want. That's what I'm trying to do with you: I'm trying to show you how you can make millions of dollars. **NUMBER TWO, these products are an extension of who you are.** They communicate things about you. They let people know who you are, what you stand for, and what your company stands for. They let you express things to your customers, to help you bond with them; you tell your story, and you get a chance to reach out to people like I'm trying to do with you right now.

NUMBER THREE, they help to establish your credibility. In the beginning, we didn't really have any credibility — or so we thought. The whole idea behind our *$2,500 Weekend* product was to interview Russ and to let him share his tips, tricks and strategies with our listeners. Recently, we moved into the real- estate market. Did we know anything about real estate? Absolutely not, so we interviewed all kinds of experts, which helps make complicated things simple and easy. We went out there and found the experts, but we also established our credibility in the minds of the customers, because they knew we were trying to reach out, to give them the information they wanted, needed, valued, and appreciated.

NUMBER FOUR: Because of all this, these products help you to create strong bonds with your customers. When I meet my best customers at seminars, they all feel like they know me and I feel like I know them. We share a lot in common. They've listened to me on these programs. They know my heart's in the right place, and I'm trying to serve them. **Number Five: These information products are perfectly matched to the customers you serve.** You're doing it for them, as I'm creating this product for you.

NUMBER SIX: They make people want to do more business with you. They separate you from the competition, and they really help bring people to you. People listen to you on your audio programs, they come to your seminars, they buy other kinds of information products from you, they like you; they know you're trying to help them, and they believe you really *can* help them, and naturally they want to do more business with you.

NUMBER SEVEN: These products lead the prospect down the path you want them to take. Establish your credibility or your authority. You can break the ice with them. Start introducing them to more of whatever it is that you have to offer.

Number Eight: Your product helps the most qualified prospects and customers in the highest way. It gives them the shortcut secrets, and that's what I'm trying to give you right now: proven strategies, insider knowledge. How many people understand that the secret to getting rich in the opportunity market is to create hard products? That's just one of the strategies that I'm sharing with you in this book. I'm reaching out to you, right now, to try to give you the insider knowledge that I've learned over the last 20 years.

> **THINK ON PAPER!** The very act of putting your ideas on paper forces you to think!

NUMBER NINE: A good information product separates you from all your competitors. When it's done correctly, your information product has zero competition, because it's an extension of you. It's your unique thumbprint. It's also a great relationship-building tool that makes people feel that they know you. It deepens your bond with established customers, and makes new prospects want to do business with you.

And NUMBER TEN: Product development is a highly creative activity that lets you clarify your thinking, lets you shape your thoughts, lets you learn as you teach. See, you can never really help somebody else without also helping yourself. So I'm trying to reach out for you on this product, I'm trying to give you some of my best ideas; but in the process, as I spent all this time writing and editing these chapters, thinking everything through very clearly, I'm learning things myself. To teach is to learn twice; one of the great philosophers said that thousands of years ago. So it helps you, but it's also something that's exciting; it's fun, it's creative. **The profit margins are also incredibly high, and the perceived value is very high for what you're offering.** In other words, developing products can make you millions of dollars. I told you about the $1 million we made with *The $2,500 Weekend*. That *Dialing for Dollars* program — it got us started, and eventually we made millions of dollars with it. But we've continued to develop more and more products, and that's the last thing I want to share with you on this section. **You've got to do something every single day to develop products.**

Ongoing product development is the secret to developing a ton of products, and you should discipline yourself to do a small amount of it every day. Every day, the first thing in the morning, my day starts out with product development. I'm spending one hour on product development each day, and it adds up to a huge arsenal of products. In doing this, you completely separate yourself from every other competitor, and it lets you attract and retain the largest number of best prospects and customers in your marketplace. **Just do it a little every day. Think about your customers and what they really want the most, and what they hate the most.** Think about what they're really seeking the most, and why they buy the things that they buy the most. Study the most successful companies in your marketplace and figure out what they're doing right, what they're doing wrong, where the gaps are in your market, and just start developing products. It doesn't have to be perfect. I've been doing this for 20 years now. I told you what a joke our first product was; it was just some thin little piece-of-crap booklet that we came out with. **We give it away in our seminars now for free, just to show people what a humble beginning it was.** It's a joke to look at it now, and yet the customers loved it. **It was raw, it was real, it was genuine, it really worked, and it was based on something that excited them. That's all that matters!**

You don't have to be perfect to produce products that connect with your customers and sell briskly. I do face-to-face seminars and create audio products all the time, but am I a professional speaker? Absolutely not. I am, however, trying to practice what I preach here. **I'm very, very focused on you, the customers. I know what I'm talking about.** My wife and I parlayed $300 into $120 million in our first 20 years, and these are the secrets that did it for us — and so what do you care if I'm not a professional speaker or writer? **You want somebody who's going to be honest and straightforward with you, who's going to give you proven methods to take you from where you are now to where you want to go.** You may be saying, "Well, I don't have any expertise," but I'm here to tell you that you *can* still create companies that provide all kinds of valuable information products.

I've told you that we're doing it in the real-estate world right now. We're interviewing all these real-estate experts, and we ask each at the end, "Who else do you know that we should be interviewing?" One expert leads us to another. We did that in the world of eBay, and we've done that with computer bulletin boards for Internet marketing. **Eventually, you *do* become an expert. But I just want to get you on the path; I want to tell you that it's more than just making money.** This is a rewarding way of life that lets you develop products and services that truly can help people. The most qualified people out there, those who are willing to put in the effort to use the ideas you share with them — those people's lives will be transformed, just like my life was.

So I want to encourage you to think about everything I've said here. **This secret really is a secret, because most people just dream of it, no more.** They would love to self-publish their stuff. They would love to produce books and audio programs, but they never do. They're always afraid, and part of that fear is that they've got to be perfect, that they aren't well qualified. **None of that matters. I promise you, if you want to do this, you can.** There are plenty of experts out there — as with the real-estate deal we're doing now — who have their own programs they want to promote. They want to develop clients and customer, so they're more than happy to spend 90 minutes or two hours with us on the phone, letting us interview them.

This is something that can make you millions and millions of dollars — and it can also provide a lot of joy and satisfaction. **It can help you completely separate yourself from every other company that's out there, because the products that you create are a piece of you.** They're an extension of who you are; they let people get to know you, and let you develop bonds with

> **B**lur the lines between your work and play.

them so you can keep the same customers coming back and buying from you for many, many years. Start getting into the routine of creating some type of information product on a daily basis. If you'll do that, ten years from now you can have a huge catalog of products that you've developed specifically for your customers, and it'll give you a high level of pride and satisfaction, the joy of accomplishment that you did something that was so productive and so creative. **All you did was to discipline yourself to do a little every day and stayed focused on serving the customers.** This can lead to a lifetime of wealth and great satisfaction for you.

CHAPTER 2

Why the Biz Opp Market Really is the Way to Go

You truly can get wealthy in the business opportunity market. This is a subject near and dear to our hearts here at M.O.R.E., Inc.; it's how we got started, and it's something that can put millions of dollars in your bank account. That's not a promise or a guarantee that it will, but I know that it *can* — because it's done it for me and for many others.

Most people want to make more money — and sure, usually they're already making *some* money, but they're working 40, 50, or 60 hours a week to get it. **That's one of the things I like about the business opportunity market: it gives you the opportunity to make the money you want, and to live the lifestyle that you want to live.** I also love the private nature of it. **Having a business that produces money without everybody knowing what you're doing is wonderful!** That's the problem with some of these multi-level marketing opportunities, and of course if you have a local business, everybody and their brother knows *exactly* what you're doing. In fact, you have to constantly pitch to people. I think that's one of the challenges to both network and retail marketing. Not only does everybody know what you're doing, but you *have* to have them know what you're doing. You have to get out there and gladhand, and you have to talk to people, and you have to network. You *want* your neighbors to know your business.

In network marketing, it can be even worse because most network marketing companies tell you that you need to practice this "three foot rule." That is, you have to talk to anybody who comes within three feet of you about your network marketing program. I've been accosted by people in malls, when I'm just standing there waiting for somebody; someone will come up and say, "Hey, what's your name?" And I introduce myself, whereupon they say, "Hey, can I tell you about this great new juice?" No, please don't, you know? These people come up to you at gas stations, and grocery stores. It's a good way to turn a lot of people off — and unfortunately, that's the nature of most network marketing opportunities. Whereas with the business opportunity market, you're able to approach people via mail or through the Internet. **You don't have to talk to anybody one-on-one if you don't want to, you're not doing any face-to-face selling, and you're not worrying about any rejection.** People can turn you down simply by not replying to your e-mail or by not clicking on your Internet link. This is one of those businesses that even shy people can get into.

You know, those of us who are really into this market are kind of spoiled. We forget sometimes just what a great business it is, especially when you compare it to the work aday world. Even for most people who start their own businesses, that dream of being self-employed soon turns into nothing but a nightmare. They're working long hours, they're working evenings and weekends, they're giving up time with their family, they're constantly traveling — and they have to learn how to become salespeople. If you want to get rich in network marketing, you better learn how to get up in front of 200-300 people and start razzlin' and dazzlin' the crowd. The people making decent money in network marketing are extremely charismatic and are able to effectively work large crowds. And of course, those are skills anybody can learn if they want — but a lot of people just don't want to. I don't blame them.

And let me make a point here that you probably don't want to hear. It tends to be something of a sore point for most of my clients, and certainly it was a sore point of mine before I made it big. Almost every time you hear a successful person interviewed, they'll say something like, "Oh, the money isn't the main thing," or "The money's not that important to me." I used to want to just throw things at the TV every time I heard someone say that! But nowadays, I find myself saying things like that to people myself, especially when I'm speaking to them in private. Because in the final analysis, it's true. **Money *is* important, don't get me wrong — but it's not the *most* important thing when it comes to business success.**

> There is so much joy that comes from the long-term effects of a life of <u>hard work</u>, <u>discipline</u>, <u>focus</u>, <u>goal setting</u>, <u>commitment</u>, and <u>daily striving to work towards your dream</u>.

Now, when you first get into the market, the real focus *is* the money, because most of us get into an opportunity because we're feeling some sort of pain — usually related to being in debt. So we're very motivated, because we're driven by our pain. If we're lucky, we like what we're doing — but in many cases we're just money motivated. I know *I* was at the beginning. I always had these dreams of becoming a millionaire, and having a beautiful home and car, and traveling, and all this fun stuff. Well, what often happens is that you start reaching your goals, and then you have to ask yourself: *What happens when I become a millionaire? What happens when I'm financially independent and have the nice home, and the cars, and the trips — what happens then, when all my motivation goes away completely, because I've reached my financial goals?*

My friend Jeff Gardner tells me that when this happened to him, he became somewhat depressed. Not clinically depressed — but he just didn't have that drive anymore, because his pain of not having enough money was gone. He had all the things he wanted in his life, so he started looking for other ways to entertain himself. He did indoor rock climbing, took up snowboarding, and took correspondence classes on photography. He was searching for something new, because that drive and motivation was gone. And what he realized, finally, is that **once you've achieved a goal, you simply have to set a new one — so that you'll have different drives and motivations within your business. As with me, that became teaching other people,** consulting with other people, helping other people gain their financial independence and freedom. That became his new motivation, his new passion.

So yes, honestly, for Jeff it really isn't about the money, because he's got enough of that. Now he uses the money as a kind of scorecard, just as I do. **Now we're driven based on our passion and love for the business. And by the way, there's certainly nothing wrong with being money-driven.** That's going to get you out of the hole and past whatever financial problem you're in right now. When you achieve success, however you define it, there's going to come a point where you're making so much money, and you've got all the things you ever wanted in your life, that your mindset is going to change. **You'll go from being money motivated to being motivated either by further growth, or by how you can help other people.** Or, you may ponder how you can gain more passion in your business, or start other businesses. **So it's just a mindset change.**

Maybe, by now, you're rolling your eyes; I can understand that. We're conditioned to expect that money does matter more than anything else, and I'm not going to tell you it doesn't. In fact, some people will go too far in the other direction, which I think is dangerous. There's a bestselling book out there that tells you, *Do what you love and the money will follow.* Well... maybe. I think that's a bit misleading, because **the real secret is to fall in love with something that's *capable* of making you a lot of money, and then the money really will follow...** because let's get real, here. Some of us love hanging out on the couch and eating Cheetos while watching TV, but who's going to pay you for that? Some of us love sitting at home and reading a good book, but with rare exceptions, no one's going to pay you for it.

So the real secret is to find something that you have a passion for, but that can also make you money. You have to get past this idea of just finding the thing you like to do the most and expecting it to profit you. Yeah, sure: Find something you're passionate about, because if you can find that passion, you're going to have that drive to make the money you want and continue building that business. **But make sure it's something that you can make good money at. This is a business, after all!**

For years, we were members of Dan Kennedy's Platinum Group — and Dan is a guy who just says whatever's on his mind and always talks straight to you. He's the most straight-talking person that I know, in fact. On more than one occasion, Dan called me an evangelist. He said, "Okay, T.J., if you wanna be an evangelist, you just go right ahead." But quite honestly, I look at that as a compliment; because **the people who do the best in the opportunity market are the ones who have a strong need or desire to reach out, to help other people, to lift people up** — to somehow motivate and inspire other people and take them from where they are now to wherever they want to be.

And when you're in the opportunity market, what you're doing is selling people money at a discount; that's another phrase I got from Dan Kennedy. **Basically, you're selling people the ability to make a lot of money — millions of dollars, potentially — for a relatively small fee.** For example, let's say you're selling a course on how to make money in network marketing for $1,000. But what is the actual *value* of that course? You're charging people a thousand bucks a pop, but if they really can make a million dollars using the information in that course, that's what you're selling them: a million dollars' worth of potential for a thousand. And yes, most people will waste that potential — but that does *not* mean the potential isn't real. The water backed up behind a dam has a huge potential to do work — but it's not going to if someone doesn't put in the relatively minor effort necessary to open the sluices to the turbines that generate the electricity.

> **STORIES SELL!** You must create powerful stories that captivate your prospects and customers. These are stories about you, your company, or your products or services.

Really, that's what you're doing in the business opportunity market: you're giving people the ability to make six or seven figures for a very small amount of money, if they're willing to invest their time and effort. **You're giving them an** *incredible potential opportunity* **for a small amount of money.**

Of course, there's a disconnect there between what it costs to present that plan and what it's worth. You could put that plan on a single audio CD, and that CD will cost you less than $1.50 to manufacture. You could ship it for under $10, and that's paying somebody to do the whole thing for you. But who cares if it costs you ten bucks? If the person who gets it can follow the exact, proven method that you used to make a million dollars, step-by-step, then that one audio CD could potentially be worth millions. **The cost that it takes you to produce something is not necessarily its value.**

About ten years ago, there was a fellow who sold a one-cassette program for $500. It didn't cost him that much to produce it, but that's how much it was worth to those who bought it. Right now, there's a fellow named Jim Straw from Dalton, Georgia, who has one e-book, an e-book based on the best of the best of the tips, tricks, and strategies Jim has learned for the last 40 years, that he sells for almost $1,000. He gets several sales a week, on average. **Think about that. An electronic book, where there's no cost to produce it.** There's no cost for distribution whatsoever. He did have the initial cost of putting it all together, but everything else is profit.

Some people would probably think, *That's criminal, how can you do that? That's the cost of an e-book?* Because again, after you put the e-book together, there is no cost. It's a digital download — so on every thousand-dollar sale, he's keeping a thousand dollars! And so I know that some people are going, *How can he do that? Has he no integrity?* But first of all, if you don't want to buy the book, you don't have to. Second, to those who do buy, the cost is worth it. Again, **you need to look at this in terms of value.** If you were to go up to somebody and say, "Okay, here's $10,000 in cash, but all I want you to pay *me* is $1,000," how quickly would they find that $1,000 in cash? Almost immediately, right? And they'd want to do that over and over again.

Well, that's basically what we're talking about. **Unfortunately, some people look at the literal cost of something instead of its value...** so for them, that million-dollar plan outlined on a McDonald's napkin is worth whatever the napkin costs, which is less than a cent. In my opinion, that's a poverty mindset — because whenever you look at the cost of things, you're looking at loss. You're saying to yourself, "Okay what is this going to *cost* me?" When you think that way, what you're really asking yourself is, "What am I going to *lose*?" Well, I always look at it this way: what is this going to *make* me?

Let's say you pay $5,000 to attend a seminar and just listen to one person speak for two full days. Would that be worth it? Some people have told me, point blank, that no matter what information was being provided at a seminar, they would never, ever in their life pay $5,000 for one. Well, I've paid $5,000 for a seminar. I've paid $10,000. **Why? Because I don't count the cost when the value is obviously much higher.** Like all the top marketers I know, I don't have this poverty mindset — I have an abundance mindset. I say, "Okay, it may cost me $5,000, but what will it make me? If it makes me $5,001, it's worth it!" And of course, some of these seminars can earn you six or seven figures if you implement what they're teaching. Again, look at the potential value versus the actual cost. If it's got what poker players call "positive expected value" (+EV), then go for it. **Change your mindset away from what you're going to lose,**

to what you're potentially going to *make*. Adopt that abundance mindset.

It's a mindset deal. Don't beat up on these people who are selling e-books for $1,000, *because they are delivering value*. The people who read those e-books and then put their strategies into action are going to get many times their investment back in value. **Don't envy those people — *join them*!** That's one of my top messages for this chapter.

In the opportunity market, there are two big things that you'll absolutely need to get very wealthy (and of course, there are a few other less-important things). **First, you have to have product knowledge — that is, you really have to understand everything about the product or service that you sell, and you have to be 100% sold on it yourself. Second, you need market knowledge. That means you have to intimately understand** everything about the people you're **trying to reach:** what their innermost wants and needs are, what the competitors are giving them, and more importantly, what the competitors are *not* giving them that you know they want the very most, so that you can fill those gaps.

> **G**reat marketers see opportunities where others cannot.

Now, out of the two, **market knowledge is the more important, because products come and go.** Market knowledge is easy enough to get; you probably have quite a lot already. I discussed this factor somewhat in the previous chapter, but I think it deserves some extra emphasis here.

If you're reading this book, you're no doubt involved in the opportunity market at some level. Even if you're not out there running your own ads and mailing your own direct mail packages, you've involved in this market as a consumer. I expect you're buying moneymaking plans, products, and services from companies like M.O.R.E., Inc., Jeff Gardner and others. **In other words,** ***you already have an intimate knowledge of the opportunity market.*** Sure, it's knowledge as a consumer — but all you have to do is flick a mental switch and you're on the other side of the cash register. Once you flick it, once you understand that the opportunity market is made up of tens of millions of people who are exactly like you, who have that same desire in their hearts — **once you really understand that, your life will be changed forever.** No longer will you be content to be a consumer. **You'll want to get on the other side of the cash register and start learning all of the other things that you have to learn to tap into this marketplace.**

One again — and this is something that we stress at our seminars over and over again — **you need to develop an intimate awareness that this is a marketplace made up of people who are** *just exactly like you are.* The more you're able to understand that, the more quickly you'll grasp a key that will lead you to riches if wielded properly. That's one of the reasons my wife Eileen and I made so many millions of dollars right off the bat. Not to discount all the help that we received from Russ von Hoelscher, Dan Kennedy, and others, **but the real key was our knowledge of the marketplace.**

You know, a lot of consumers in the business opportunity market want to start a business — they want to rush out and sell things to carpet cleaners and doctors and lawyers, and they want to go to these people who they think have money, instead of staying in their own market, in the business opportunity market — where they have an intimate knowledge. **This is a mistake.** If you're not a doctor or lawyer or carpet cleaner, how can you know what they really want, except in a very general sort of way? **Sell what you know.** If you see an opportunity that makes you excited, that really gets your passion going, that you want to buy — well, you can safely assume that there are probably tens of thousands, hundreds of thousands, even *millions* of people just like you who are excited about that same type of an opportunity.

Now, if you're thinking like a consumer, you might buy that opportunity. **If you're thinking like a marketer of business opportunities, what you would do instead is take that concept that excites you so much and create your own similar opportunity.** That's really how people get rich in the business opportunity market. Yes, you can make money as a consumer. You can buy a course on network marketing, or eBay, or real estate, and put it into action and make some cash. **The people who are making the real money are the marketers of these business opportunities,** those are supplying this huge market of business opportunity seekers with the products, services, and opportunities that they really want and need to solve their financial problems.

And I know that all this may seem completely overwhelming. You may say, "I don't even know how to get started." **Not to be glib, but really, the best way to get started is just to get started.** You can begin by placing small ads in specialty publications, or find other venues that will accept advertisements for moneymaking biz opps. Sometimes it won't cost you anything to do this. For example, when my colleague Jeff Gardner got started, he didn't have that much money. He knew the market, he knew what products would sell because he knew what he liked to buy, but he didn't have a big advertising budget. So he did some free advertising first, and then some very low-cost classified and small display advertising — and it got him started. **The key is to dip your toe in the water; get started, even if it's at a very small level, and start being a marketer of business opportunities versus a constant consumer of business opportunities.**

You already have the market knowledge, and that's incredibly important, because again, **you really are selling to people who are just like you.** They're people that you understand at a deep level. Every time I go back and look at my own story, I realize anew that one of the reasons why Eileen and I were so successful is because we deeply understood what people wanted in this marketplace, We knew what they liked, what they didn't like, what their sources of frustration were; and we used all that knowledge to create products and services that we knew would get people excited. **Because again, we knew what excited us and we knew what the market was lacking, because we were consumers for so many years.**

The second thing that we did was to get help from experts who had the knowledge and the experience that we lacked. The first expert who helped us was Russ von Hoelscher. He saw some of the first little display ads that we were running in moneymaking magazines, and actually ordered our little booklet, *Dialing for Dollars* — and he liked it. He sent us a little brochure and just said, "Look, guys, I've seen your program. I like what you're doing, and I think I can help."

Well, by then we were already

> STAY VERY CLOSE TO YOUR CUSTOMER. Know your customers _better_ than they know themselves. How? By thinking about them all the time and realizing that _the real reasons_ they buy are mostly unconscious.

raking in the dough from little profit makers! We were generating about $16,000 a month, with about a 35% profit margin every single month. **Our banker told us, "Eileen and T.J., I've never seen any company make 35-40% net profit month after month right out of the gate."** He had 30 years of experience, too. That, again, is testament to the profits that can be made here. We were selling a little program that didn't look like very much. The booklet is poorly written, just a little brochure filled with typographical errors. It's kind of embarrassing to look at now... and yet, that's what launched the millions of dollars we've made.

And even though we were making some good money, we wanted more! So Russ took us by the hand, worked with us, and helped us. He had over 20 years of knowledge and experience when he first got started with us. And then Dan Kennedy came along about five years later, and thanks to the help they gave us, we ended up bringing in over $100 million in 21 years.

But again, it was our knowledge of the marketplace that was our foundation. Then we went out there and got the right kind of help, the right kind of support, the right kind of guidance from these experts who had gone before us. They had learned the solutions to most of the problems that we had yet to figure out. They helped us solve these problems, they introduced us to their contacts, they revealed little-known tips, tricks, and strategies to us... in short, they gave us the shortcuts that we needed to go out there and make millions of dollars. **That's why we do the same today for new up-and-coming marketers.** It's absolutely imperative to have help from people who have been where you want to go.

Jeff Gardner attributes his years of struggling early on to simply not having anybody to learn from. Now, he was in the business and was trying to see what other people were doing; but he lacked their experience and knowledge, **so most of the learning he did in those first 10 years was all through trial and error.** It was him putting out ads, not getting any response, changing the ads, trying something else. Writing a product, putting it out there, not getting any sales. It was getting all those bruises and bumps trying to figure out the market.

So that's one of the things that Jeff tells people today: "You can certainly do this all by yourself, but I guarantee you it's going to take you 10-20 times more time, effort, energy, and money than if you'll just find an expert in the field, let them hand you a formula on a silver platter, and just put it into action, A to Z." **When people come me or Jeff for guidance, that's usually what they're after: the real shortcut to riches.** They say, "Look, let's just cut out all the B.S. You just tell me what the real shortcut is." And the truth is, there's a lot of stuff to know, and a lot of it's based on sacrifice and hard work. But when they ask me that, I tell them, **"Find somebody who's successful, find some successful business models, and just copy what they're doing."**

We don't mean that you should copy their sales letters or their products; **I'm not promoting plagiarism here. But what you *should* do is model their successful business.** Finding a mentor who can tell you all the secrets, who can tell you all the mistakes they made and how to avoid them, can literally save you tens of thousands of dollars (or more) in wasted money, in wasted time, in wasted energy. So absolutely: if you want to make a lot of money in the business opportunity market without *wasting* a lot of money, and take years off your learning curve, **the best thing you can do is connect to a mentor who's going to tell you exactly how to do it.**

Business levels the playing field. Anyone with a strong desire to get rich and the willingness to do whatever it takes — CAN GET RICH!

Approached positively and with a little help, you *can* make a killing in the opportunity market. **It takes some hard work, but it's a real possibility;** I'm one of the best examples of this fact. I started with $300 (seriously, three hundred bucks) and I've made over $114 million since. I'm here to tell you that it can be done, that it is *being* done. Want to make a seven-figure salary? You can. All of your friends and relatives who have never made even six figures in their life will all tell you, *Oh no, there's no possible way you could ever make over a million dollars a year. Not you.* **Well, I'm here to tell you that you** *can.*

You can do it. I've done it, you can do it, and there are plenty of people in the opportunity market who are doing it right now, completely legitimately. **And where's that money coming from? From the tremendous demand in this marketplace.** Depending on the expert you're talking to, there are literally millions people out there with a hunger to make more money. America is the land of opportunity; in the 1850s, Ralph Waldo Emerson said "America is another name for opportunity." This is an American thing that's never going to change. There were people a hundred years ago selling moneymaking plans and programs; there are going to be people getting rich 100 years from now selling moneymaking plans and programs. **This is a market that's here to stay. There's** *always* **something new.**

Let's look at the long-term. Most people think nothing of spending $40,000 or $50,000 to go through college, so they can get out of college and go get a $40,000-or-$50,000 a year job and live in the suburbs where every house is exactly the same. If you had a little bit too much to drink on a Saturday night, you might pull up in your neighbor's garage or driveway, thinking that it's your house, because all the houses are so alike. People will spend $40,000-$60,000 to go through 6-8 years of education so they can knock down maybe $100,000 a year someday — if they play their cards right. **But with the opportunity market, we're talking about something that can make people very wealthy, and it all comes from nothing but tremendous long-term demand.**

Most people don't get it, though. They'll laugh at you if you try to explain this to them; or worse, they'll think you're trying to cheat people. And let me tell you a little story about people laughing at you, courtesy of Jeff Gardner. His friends and family thought he was crazy when he got into the business opportunity market as a teenager. His parents put a lot of pressure on him to go get a college degree. So he agreed, went off to college, and got into a lot of debt — college is very expensive. He got a degree in Elementary Education, so he was certified to teach kindergarten through ninth grade.

He didn't really enjoy it. He loved the kids, but not the politics and some of the other stuff going on in the school system. Jeff's parents wanted him to get that degree to be safe; but at the same time, in his spare time, he was in the business opportunity market, spending lots of money and reading lots of books, going to seminars and whatnot, trying to figure out this market. Ultimately, what happened was that Jeff was $40,000 in debt after he got out of college, and guess what — he now had a degree, after four years of his time spent. And guess what? He was now qualified to have a $28,000-a-year job. Woohoo! Well, that wasn't really his dream. So he continued to work in the business opportunity market, even though, again, his friends and family were laughing at him. Well, I guess the joke's on them now!

Jeff loves his family and friends very much — but they were flat-out wrong. He's very successful in the business opportunity market. Now he has days where he makes $30,000, $40,000, $50,000, even $70,000 — in a single *day*, which completely blows away what he would've made in an entire year as a teacher! That ought to blow your mind! So when people say, "Oh, it can't be done," Jeff can look 'em in the eye and say, "Yes it *can* be done. I'm living proof that it can be done. **Even with people laughing at you, with all this debt from going to college hanging over your head, it can be done."** You just have to know how to do it, and you have to know and believe that it can be done, realizing that other people are doing it — because believe me, plenty of people really are. Not just Jeff and I, but lots of people.

Once you believe that and know it in your heart, you can achieve it. Use what you know as a business-opportunity consumer, and find a mentor who can get you there faster without spending so much money. **Believe in yourself, work hard, step up to the plate — and hit a millionaire grand slam.**

I'm just an ordinary joe from Middle America, a hometown boy from Kansas. **If I can do it, I know that you can, too.**

3

Establishing Your USP

In this chapter, we're going to talk about building a Unique Selling Position — what's also known in the industry as a Unique Selling Proposition or, more succinctly, a USP. If you have no idea what a USP is, then what you learn in this chapter alone will be worth every penny you paid for this book. Even if you already know all about USPs, by the time we're done here you'll have learned a lot you didn't know already, and you'll have supercharged your understanding of this valuable marketing strategy.

Ask yourself this one question as you read this chapter: why do your clients buy from you instead of your competitors? If you can't answer that question, it means one of two things: either you're offering your clients a unique set of advantages that you've never bothered to identify, or you offer *no* unique advantages, so you're lucky to have any business in the first place. If that's the case, there's no compelling reason for your customers to keep doing business with you. Therefore, anytime your competitors offer your customers a unique

advantage, they can steal those customers away.

You can't let that happen! In this chapter, I'm going to show you how to build your own Unique Selling Position: a USP that completely separates you from all of the other competitors in your market, and makes people want to keep doing business with you over and over again. So, please: read carefully, and take plenty of notes.

What a USP Is, and Why It's Important

Ask a dozen marketing experts what a USP is, and you'll get a dozen answers — but they'll have a lot in common. At its most basic, **a USP is a clear statement of the unique benefits your customers get from doing business with you. It's something that sets you apart from your competition.** No matter what field you're in, all your competitors are usually saying the same thing. A USP is something — a benefit, an idea, a concept — that helps you say something your competitors don't, so that when people look at your business, it stands out against the rest of the field and looks unique to their eyes.

The most unique USP possible would be to have a product that everybody wants and nobody else has. The only problem there is that 99.99% of businesses *don't* have that. They've got plenty of competition. It doesn't matter if you're a chiropractor, a dentist, an attorney, a plumber, or an air conditioner repairman: whatever you're doing, chances are you've got competition up the kazoo. **A USP is important because it defines you and your company, and gives potential customers a very compelling reason — or even several reasons — why they should favor you over all those competitors.**

You can **look at a USP as simply what you do better or differently than everybody else. In most cases, you should be able to get your USP down to a few words.** Here are three great examples I picked up from a website. Burger King says, "Have it your way!" Enterprise Car Rental says, "We'll pick you up." Bounty Paper Towels call themselves "The Quicker Picker-Upper." The best USP is a condensed catchphrase that tells your customers why they should do business with you instead of your

> **P**laying it safe is no guarantee against misfortune.

competition. Your answer has to telegraph a very clear and direct benefit to your prospect or customer, in a concise, distinct, fulfilling way.

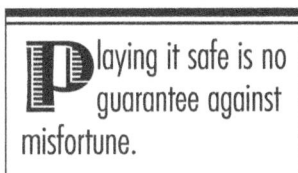

For example, if you were to say, "Melts in your mouth, not in your hands!" everyone would know you were talking about M & M's. That's a classic USP, and it's sold millions of dollars worth of candy over the years. A good USP like that one stays with a person, etched into both their subconscious and their conscious mind, so when they walk away and later think about buying a product in that particular category, they'll think of you first. Here are a few more great examples: take Avis Rent-A-Car. They couldn't be #1 in their market — that was Hertz — so they came up with this USP: "We're #2. We try harder!" And here's Federal Express: "When it absolutely, positively has to be get there overnight." And then there's the old USP for Domino's Pizza, which is my favorite, though the government actually court-ordered them to stop using it because of a lawsuit. It was so brilliant: "Fresh hot pizza in 30 minutes or less!" What could be clearer than that?

The USP, then, is whatever you can offer that your best prospects or customers want the most that nobody else has —

and it's up to you to discover or create that. I'm going to show you how in this chapter. But just as important, I'm going to show you exactly what a USP is *not*. If you flip through the Yellow Pages or a newspaper advertising section, you'll see plenty of examples of what a USP is not: and that's just your name, your address, your telephone number, how many years you've been in business, the fact that you're "family-owned," and so on. That's what you see in most advertising — but that's not a USP. It doesn't telegraph any benefit. You need to give people not what they *need*, but what they *want*. And **what people want is to solve their problems or to fulfill their desires, as quickly, easily, and painlessly as possible.**

Taming the Wild USP

Now we'll get into the meat-and-potatoes of what a USP really is, and how to find the one that's right for you. This isn't an easy process for the inexperienced marketer. First of all, how do you get started? That's usually a little daunting, because you may not be sure exactly what a USP is, although you should have some general idea by now. **The first question you should always ask yourself is, "What needs are going unfulfilled in my industry, or in this segment of my target market? What problems need to be fixed?" The second question is, "What great value, service, or benefit will people receive from my business that will justify them doing business with me?"**

So… is a USP a slogan? It is indeed, in its most basic sense, but even then you have to gather together all your raw material before you try to put it into a statement. **An easy way to do that is to compile a Claims Matrix.** A Claims Matrix is a chart, a visual representation of what's out there, who's saying what, and what's available. Frankly, very few companies are in a position so unique that they don't have direct competition. Even if you have a unique service that everybody needs and no one else provides… well, you're a very rare bird, and you won't be in that position for very long. If you're trying something new, it's either going to succeed because of its uniqueness, or you're going to discover that the product is unique because there was no demand for it in the first place. Even if you do succeed, you'll have imitators very quickly. Imitation may be the sincerest form of flattery, but it can hurt you severely if it steals away dollars that should be yours.

Here's how you create a Claims Matrix to get all the raw data to work from. You can do it on paper, on a computer spreadsheet, or even in your head if you can handle all the data that way. **Down one side of the chart, list all the benefits and features you can think of that pertain to your product or service. Include all the features and benefits your competition is claiming.** That might be that they have 24 stores and locations, free delivery, same-day service, or whatever. You should include as many as you can think of.

Then, across the top of the chart, write the names of all your competitors. Once you've done that, go down the chart and put a checkmark next to each feature or claim that's being made by each competitor. So, if it's fast delivery and there are three competitors who make that claim, you put the checkmark in the spaces for those three businesses. Go right on down the line, and spend a little while doing this. You'd better come back after a day or so, because more features and benefits will dawn on you. **When you complete this simple task, you'll have a visual representation of what other people are doing, and you'll very likely see big, open spaces where no competitor is making a claim.** These open spaces offer a whole list of ideas you can claim; they're the raw data you can work from to create your own USPs. And don't be scared to have more than one, especially if you have different divisions within your company.

Here's one of the prime lessons you should take away from this chapter: *even if you're not unique, you can be unique in saying what no one else is saying.* Once you've put together a nice list of benefits and features, you can translate any of those features into additional benefits.

> The way to sell the *unfamiliar* is to link it with the *familiar.*

As you go down that list, you'll read a feature and ask yourself, "So what?" For instance, here's a typical claim: "We have the most locations." So what? "Well, that means you're never more than ten minutes away from one of our stores." So what? "That means you're only 20 minutes from having food at home that's still hot and fresh." Aha! There's your *real* benefit.

Keep going down the list. Suppose someone claims, "We have the largest inventory." So what? He has the biggest selection; what does that mean? "That means you can always find the hard-to-find items that the other stores don't carry." *Now* you have a clue.

Once you complete your Claims Matrix, you have the raw data to begin crafting your USP. Your list can be very long in the beginning, but then you can start editing it down until you end up with a single statement that says everything you want to say. It **tells the customer, "Here's why you should do business with me; this is a unique benefit you'll get."** You're claiming something in the marketplace that none of your competition is claiming. That will help you get started. This is an ongoing process, and it may take you a few days just to get some preliminary ideas about what you want to do. But that's okay; this is something you need to hammer out right now before you even open your doors. Figure out what your point of difference is going to be. What are you going to offer to your customers and prospects that's different from everybody else? You've got to answer this question, and it has to be something that will compel them to do business with you rather than your competitors. That said, keep in mind that a USP isn't necessarily set in stone. It evolves; you're constantly asking yourself these questions, so your USP is a process rather than a static thing that just pops into your head full-grown and never changes. **Your best ideas will come from the time you put into process.**

Here's one of the things that makes this process so useful: if you talk to most businesspeople about developing a Claims Matrix and adding up all the benefits and features, they'll look at you like you're speaking a foreign language. That's because hardly anybody puts in the effort to do this, or even knows they should. **This is your real advantage here.** It's your edge in the marketplace: the fact that most people won't take the time to do this.

The best evidence of that is that most businesses are saying the same thing — they're "me too" businesses. Drive through any town, and you'll see hundreds of little businesses. Not that there's anything wrong with that, but these little businesses are all the same: little gift shops, hole-in-the-wall restaurants, antique stores, and the like. It's obvious that so many people have poured their hearts, lives, and all their assets into opening a business, without ever wondering how that business is going to succeed. They do no market research; they have no idea why people would do business with them, as opposed to all the other shops that are offering the same thing. They just open their doors and say, "I offer that, too."

You've also got to take care to avoid marketing pitfalls in creating your USP. Let's say you decide to carve out a niche in the printer cartridge industry. It's a very competitive market, so you might decide to build your USP around your price. Here's where you have to be careful, because the prices are more or less the same throughout the industry for specific printer cartridges. Quality? That's about the same, too. Delivery? Yep, that's about the same. So how do you differentiate yourself? How do you create a USP that gives you that competitive advantage? One individual did this: he sent out an email reminder when it was about time to replace a cartridge one of his customers had purchased.

There's always something there that research will uncover if you do it correctly, especially if you do your matrix chart first. Often, business owners and marketers talk about the benefits to the buyer, but we fail to appreciate that the important part is taking that feature and showing the customer how buying a product conveys the benefit to them. That's what your USP does. It takes the person from asking, "Should I or shouldn't I buy this product?" to a point where they say, "I can't live without this product, because it benefits me *this* way."

You May Think That's a USP, But It's Not

Wanna know a secret? Here it is: *You only have to be a little better than everybody else in order to get all the business you can handle.* One reason is that most businesses out there don't have a clue what a USP is, let alone *have* one. **I'd say at least**

98% of businesses out there, in any field, have no real understanding of the concept of the USP. They're not telegraphing any benefits to their prospects or customers. They hang a sign in the window that says "OPEN," and feel that's a compelling enough reason to get people stampeding through the doors. It just doesn't happen.

In order to understand what truly comprises a USP, you need to understand what a USP isn't. When I look at the ads in the newspaper, the Yellow Pages, and other venues — even the mail — I see advertisers talking about quality and service. Here's a common refrain: "We offer exceptional quality and service!" Well, holy-moly, that's going to make me run down and buy everything you have! Yeah, right. Frankly, **in most cases "quality" and "service" are empty words. They're repeated over and over by so many businesses that they've become meaningless to the consumer.** It's too often the case that the businesses using these empty words just aren't delivering on their promises. And here's the kicker: often the employees of those businesses have no idea what the company's USP is, so they don't even realize they aren't delivering on their promises. They're totally clueless — totally disconnected from the USP.

> **H**appiness is... a never-ending stream of positive cash-flow!

That's not to say that simple things like quality, price, and service can't make good USPs; they can, but you have to use them very, very carefully. Because they're so simple, they're often weak, and present hazards that can kill a young business. Here's a great USP, *if* you can back it up: your price is the lowest. **It's a dangerous USP, too, because if your price is the lowest, your profit margin is small, and that may hurt you.**

You can only make it with this USP if you have a product that you really can cut the price on, so you can cut down the competition along with your price. This works like magic if it's still profitable. McDonald's does it with burgers, and Wal-Mart does it with discount consumer goods. Most of us can't make a dangerous USP like this work, and I'll tell you why later on.

High quality is also good USP material, but you have to explain, exactly, everything that people want to know about the quality. You can't just use those empty words I mentioned before. Greater choice can be a USP, but only if you really do have a tremendous selection. **Exceptional service is always a good USP, as long as you define your service and make it known exactly what it is you're offering.** In other words, if you offer help after the sale, you tell your customers, "Here's what we'll do for you after the sale, and how we'll be there to help you if anything comes up." A superior guarantee can be a powerful USP, but it should be a long guarantee, without a lot of escape clauses, that people can readily see is advantageous to them.

Danger, Will Robinson!

Quality, price, and service: these are all USPs that are viable, but they're weak. That is, they can work under certain circumstances, but you really, really have to know what you're doing to use them well. **In my opinion, lowest price is absolutely the worst of all the workable USPs you can try.** I'm speaking from experience here, because 20 years ago, when I started my first business, that was my USP: I was a cheap date. I was the lowest-priced provider in my market — and I'm telling you, it's horrible.

First of all, any idiot can offer the lowest price. It takes no imagination whatsoever; it takes no creativity. It's dumb for a lot of reasons, but part of the reason it's dumb is that with all of the unforeseen costs in business, **you need to charge premium rates just so you can afford to develop the kind of infrastructure that's needed to support the levels of service that keep your customers coming back.** In my case, I was the lowest-priced carpet cleaner in my market. I couldn't afford to upgrade my equipment. My level of service was poor, because I was always running from one job to the next, and my whole business model required me to spend as little time at each job as possible. So everything suffered.

Here's another reason that offering the absolute rock-bottom lowest price is a bad idea, short and to the point: **it can backfire on you.** Some people will choose a product or service on price, and that's always the way they're going to shop — period. But **if they're willing to buy on price, they'll leave you on price, too.** Others shop on price because they don't know any better. The first question they ask when they call a new company is what the price is, because they don't know any other question to ask. Most businesses can't give them a better question to ask, because they don't operate with a USP.

I can't emphasize enough how important a USP is to your business. While it's true that most people shop according to price at least occasionally, they're often willing to choose goods and services based on benefits. If you can provide a USP that gives your prospect a reason to do business with you instead of the low-priced guy, they're going to choose you. **With a strong USP, you can easily justify higher prices and get them, because you're not competing on price: you've got other things to offer.** The cream is going to rise to the top: you're going to get better customers who are easier to deal with, who

have money and are willing to spend it, if you offer things that
appeal to those customers.

Build It, and They Will Come

**In this section, I'm going to tell you how to built a
powerful USP that will attract customers for years to come.**
I'll start with three secrets that will practically force your
customers to do business with you instead of your competition.
These are conceptual items that, if you'll keep them in mind as
you develop your USP, will help you fashion one that does the
job in a potent and consistent manner.

Number One: The More Unique You Are, The Better

There's a reason it's called a
Unique Selling Position. At its root, a
USP is really just what that separates
you from your competition, whether
that's one thing or several; it's what
makes a person choose to do business

> **B**etter to
> strengthen your
> back than to lighten
> your load!

with you rather than the guy down the street. That means you
have to think about what makes you different from the next guy
selling the same thing.

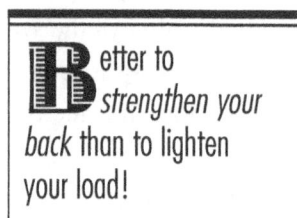

Let's say you sell a certain type of widget, and there are
hundreds of people in your market selling that widget. There are
still ways you can set yourself apart from your competitors. This
could be anything from a catchy name or slogan, to how fast you
ship your product. Maybe everyone else takes four to five days to
ship the widget — but you do it in 24 hours. These are just a few
off-the-cuff examples: there are all kinds of things you can come
up with if you put a little skull-sweat into it. **Your USP can even**

be so unique that it's controversial. That makes it newsworthy. That, in turn, leads to free publicity. If you have the right USP in place, it's going to give you a competitive advantage, because you're the company the media is focusing on — and as a result, you're the business that your target market is going to focus on.

Here's a related point. **As much as you want to attract the right people to your business, it's equally as important to repel the *wrong* people.** What that means is, you've got to have enough courage to not worry about ticking off the wrong people. You're looking for just one type of person; that's all you care about, and that's who your message is aimed at. The more controversial it is, assuming that you don't repel the kind of people that you're looking for, the better. Many businesses, I think, are preoccupied with trying to be lukewarm. They're trying to attract everybody, and their messages have no real power to their potential customers whatsoever. It's like jumping up and down in the ocean instead of in a puddle.

Number Two: Know Your Competitors Better Than They Know Themselves

You can't assume that just because you sell the same widget as your competitors, you understand how those competitors operate. Take Sam Walton, the founder of Wal-Mart; he knew better. When he was starting out, he spent more time in K-Mart than most K-Mart managers! **He knew that the best way to make Wal-Mart successful was to know the competition extremely well — to know it inside and out.** He spent months learning how they did business, what their prices were, and the products they sold — and in the process, he got kicked out of several K-Marts. Obviously, that didn't stop him.

If you have a physical storefront, you need to visit other stores selling the same types of products to the same types of customers, or at least stores selling related products. **You need to spend time in the store of anyone you consider a direct competitor.** Talk to their employees: if you can do it and they don't know who you are, that's great. But if they're smart and they're running their business right, they know who you are — so you might have to send someone else in to do some covert operations for you. **If you're an Internet business and don't have a physical storefront, you can do this online as well;** and it may even be easier, because to a large extent, it's anonymous. Spend plenty of time looking at other websites that sell the same kinds of products to the same types of customers. **Spend some time on Google or Yahoo doing research.** Search for the kinds of products you think your customers will be searching for when they find your website. **If you're using Pay Per Click advertising on the search engine, spend lots of time searching the same phrases that you're advertising, in order to see what other people who are running the same keywords are advertising.**

Knowing your competition, however you do it, is the best market research you'll ever do, and probably the least expensive, so it gives you the best return on your investment. Look at their literature, look at their processes, know what they're doing so you can do it better and faster and easier for the consumer. **That's inexpensive education that can give you an unfair advantage over the competition.** Shopping with them can also help you — so go ahead, order one of their products. How fast do you get it? What's in the package when you get it? What are they offering as an upsell or a back-end? How do they handle customer service complaints? How do they handle returns? You can get a wealth of information about your competition simply by ordering one of their products, or making a phone call inquiring about it.

Number Three: Be Specific About the Benefits You Offer

Generally speaking, being general is generally not a good way, in general, to come up with a USP. Did you get that? Obviously, I threw "general" in there several times to make the point that your USP can't be generic. *It's got to be specific.* **The reason a good USP works is because it makes your customer choose to do business with you over your competitors.** It makes people want to seek you out. A broad USP can't do this: it doesn't provide enough punch to get your customer to do business with you.

> *S*trive to become the competitor you would hate to compete against!

Look at Domino's Pizza, which had the best USP ever until the law made them change it: "Fresh, Hot Pizza Delivered In 30 Minutes Or Less. Guaranteed." **That USP contained four elements:**

- It 's fresh. (A lot of pizza isn't; it's anything but fresh.)
- It's hot.
- It's delivered within 30 minutes.
- That's guaranteed, or it's free.

It doesn't say the pizza tastes good, by the way. I think that's important. However, this simple statement is very clear, very compelling, and leaves nothing to the imagination. It delivered a specific benefit that used to separate Domino's from all the other pizza joints.

Be forewarned, however, that with specificity comes a built-in problem. **Your USP can come back to haunt you if you aren't careful, when you construct it, to make certain that you're able to deliver on your promises.** If you advertise the "fastest delivery in town" and your delivery is slow, that works against you. People who never paid attention to the speed of your delivery before will notice it now, and then they won't trust you. If you make a promise, make certain it's a promise your business can support; otherwise, you're better not to mention it at all. Too many companies, in presenting their USP, will add features that sound good but that they're not capable of delivering. That doesn't advance your business at all: in fact, it's just the reverse. It's suicide.

Let's look at Domino's again. If they hadn't been able to deliver pizza in 30 minutes, you would have been unhappy. But if you'd called a regular pizza delivery shop and it took 45 minutes or an hour to get there, you would have been perfectly satisfied, because that was normal service. **Once you make a promise and it raises that expectation, failure to deliver puts you in an unfavorable light.** So you have to make certain that your USP is understood clearly in its statement, that you can deliver on that USP, and more importantly, that everyone working for you knows that it's a statement you're making publicly, and that they're expected to comply with it. That's your responsibility as a business owner. If you're writing the ads, running the business, and responsible for the cash flow, you've got to make sure that your employees are in tune with your marketing message.

Refine Your USP

Here's something I want to reiterate. Your USP, whatever you come up with, isn't set in stone. **The right USP might not even come immediately; and even if it does, it may take some tinkering to get it just right.** Here's an interesting story that makes that point, one that my good friend Don Bice heard from the original Advertising Manager for Federal Express. Their classic tagline, "When it absolutely, positively has to get there overnight," took them a while to come up with — but it's made them tons of money. Here's what happened: they'd been having meeting after meeting, trying to work out a good USP, and the early efforts weren't working at all. It seems their Shipping Manager happened to be dropping some things off at one meeting, so they turned to him and said, "We're struggling with how to position our service and sell it to people." He said, "Oh, that's easy! You use us when it absolutely, positively has to get there overnight." And they said, "That's it!"

You never know where that inspiration will come from. Sometimes it comes right from your customers. **One of the secrets to developing great USPs is to hone in on the problems your customers are having, and some of the challenges they face on a daily basis.** All this is work; there's no question about it. It really does take a lot of time and effort, and it's probably not going to come overnight. But once you find that competitive advantage, you can build your entire marketing effort around it.

C'mon, Everybody Does It

An easy way to come up with your own USP is to look closely at your own company. It's funny, **but you can actually**

create a USP not by doing something differently than all your competitors, but by advertising things that *everybody* does in the marketplace but that your customers don't know about. For example, let's say you do something behind the scenes that your customers never know about, and let's say everyone else in the same marketplace does the exact same thing. You can stand up and say, "Look, this is how we do it. This is the care that we take. This is how we process orders. This is how we handle *your* order." Just by bringing that to the forefront, all of a sudden you've got a USP. Any of your competitors can say, "We do that too!" But if they do, all of a sudden they become the "me too" person, following *you*.

Here's an excellent story of how this works. In 1919 Claude Hopkins, a famous copywriter and marketing expert, was hired by Schlitz Beer. At the time, Schlitz was in something like tenth or fifteenth place in beer sales. They were desperate to boost their sales, so they hired Hopkins. He went in and asked all sorts of questions about what they did in their business, so they walked him through the factory and showed him the brewing process. He was shown how they washed the beer bottles

> The heart rules the mind! (That's why we must sell to their emotions!)

repeatedly, how carefully they chose the yeast, and all the copper kettles and other equipment they used. He was absolutely fascinated by the entire process, so he went to the people at Schlitz and said, "Look, why aren't you telling people about this? This is absolutely amazing! People would love this!" The Schlitz people replied, "But everybody else does the exact same thing." And Claude Hopkins pointed out, **"Yes, but nobody *knows* that. If you use your marketing to tell everyone how you brew your beer, it'll put you above**

and beyond everybody else. You'll be the first in this category, even though your competitors do these things too."

The Schlitz people did what Hopkins told them. They told people how beer was made, and in six months' time Schlitz was the best-selling beer in America. Did they have to change anything they did? No; **all they did was tell their customers about something they were already doing for them. They made the product interesting. It's a common product in a very competitive market, but they got around that by telling people what most brewers would assume everybody already knew. They brought it to the forefront, and that became their USP.** You see, sometimes you've got to educate your customers. You have to teach them what makes you special; don't just take it for granted. Then dramatize those facts to make them appealing to people so that it really *does* interest them, and they'll appreciate that.

That's why when you're doing your research, you should think about whatever it is you're already doing just like everybody else, but that maybe nobody knows about. **If you tell your customers about it, it sounds like inside information, or a revelation, or something new and different, maybe even a breakthrough** — *even if everybody else in your field is doing it.*

You're Selling What Now?

Here's something that many people never even consider when developing their USP. Obviously you're selling a product or a service, and you know what that is. But here's how it fits into crafting a USP. **You have to ask yourself, "What am I *really* selling?**

A perfect example is a company I know of that markets an office prospecting system. This is a management and organization service that shows you how to prospect for new clients, how to handle the clients once they're in your system, and how to get all the employees on the same page as to how this all works. That was how they marketed the product at first, plain and simple. Then at some point they asked themselves, "What are we *really* selling?"

Here's the USP they came up with. The headline for their ad was, "It puts your office on autopilot so you can spend the afternoon playing golf." Why would they do such a thing? Because they took time to back away and take a good look at their market. They asked themselves, "Who's most likely to give us money for what we're offering?" They discovered that many of the people who use this kind of system are golfers, who are looking for any excuse to get out of the office, hold all their messages, and get out on the golf course. When they realized this, they crafted their USP to target those people, and they recreated their product. In other words, they're no longer selling this unique system with all the software that does this and that and has all these wonderful features. **They're selling golf time.** Their whole selling point is that it frees you up and puts everything on autopilot so you can go play golf. **It's a great example of how you should deconstruct what your service or product is and ask yourself, what are you *really* selling?**

A Few Other Options to Consider

I think making things risk-free can be a great USP. For example, a company called Investment Rarities in Minnesota offers a two-year, money-back guarantee when you buy gold bouillon or gold coins from them — which is ideal if the market takes a downturn. Seaside Buick in San Diego offers another great example. When you buy a car from most dealers, you lose thousands of the dollars the instant you drive it off the lot — but what Seaside Buick does is offer a five-day money-back guarantee. For most products and services, five days doesn't count for much; but when you're buying a new car, it counts big-time! You take the car, you drive it anywhere you want for five days, and if you didn't like something about it, you can bring it back and get your money back in full.

My company, M.O.R.E., Inc., produces information products. **In our marketplace, which is loaded with skepticism, one of the USPs we used for years was a lifetime money-back guarantee, until our lawyer made us change it —** he told us it wasn't legal. For years, that was the deal our company offered: if you weren't happy with the product anytime within your lifetime or ours, you could get your money back — no questions asked. It blew the customers away, because they were used to dealing with lots of hassles with other companies whenever they tried to get their money back, even after 10 or 20 days, let alone years after they made the purchase!

Offering special incentives is another great way to refine your USP. Give people something extra. This works especially well if your competitors are selling the exact same products as you. **Another good USP is to zero in on the needs of your market.** If you're a sporting goods store, tell your customers that you have all the products they need for fishing, hunting, golf, or archery, or that you specialize in serving people with special health needs.

> Y**ou must enter the conversation that's already in their mind.**
> — *Robert Collier*

Here's another thing to keep in mind: try to get your USP in everything that describes what you do. For example, you can clearly telegraph a benefit, or at least what it is that you're selling, through the name on your business cards. When somebody asks you what do you do, describe what you do. Turn *that* into a USP. Don't just say, "I provide financial services," if that's what it might be. **Figure out what you're really selling, find the benefits that you can telegraph to that customer or prospect, and use that to describe what you do. You don't need to use catchy, cute, clever phrases in your USP or business name — everybody else does that.**

Instead of playing around with words, **create a name for your business that telegraphs the major benefit of what you're offering, so people don't have to scratch their heads and wonder.** Make it so that when they see you listed in the Yellow Pages, they can determine, just from the title of your business, exactly what it is that you're offering. If you're creating products, make sure that the product name telegraphs your USP and makes that benefit clear. Promotions work the same way. If you want to name the promotion, try to integrate your USP into the name of that promotion so people don't have to figure it out on their own. I'm not trying to say that your customers are stupid, but they'll appreciate it if you make life a little bit easier for them.

It's easy to get caught up in being the business owner and to forget what it's like to be the customer. What you need to do is take off the business-owner hat for just a moment, put on a consumer's hat, and pretend you've got a problem your customer wants solved. Write down the things people might be looking for. What's their exact problem? What's the exact end result they want? What do they have going on in their minds when they're looking for the product or service you're providing? In doing that, you're going to achieve some insight you didn't have before.

If you're so close to the business that you can't do this yourself, it wouldn't hurt to talk to some of your consumers; or you might be able to talk to some friends who've used your product and services. **You have to get into that customer's mindset;** don't keep working from your own mindset, saying to yourself, "Well, they *should* want this," and, "They *should* want that," and, "They *should* be interested in this." What they *should* want doesn't matter. It's what they *do* want that actually matters. **Once you find out what they *do* want, you can build your USP around that.**

Cop a Realistic Attitude About Your USP

Remember this painful fact: not everyone is as enamored with your business as you are. You may love your company and your products, but you also have to realize that we live in a busy culture that's saturated with marketing. People are busy; they've got their heads full of all kinds of different things, and the bottom line is this: **most people just don't give a damn about your business.** That's the one thing a lot of businesspeople never stop to consider, and sure, it's understandable. Our companies are our livelihoods; they're extensions of ourselves. We love what we do, and so naturally we suffer from the delusion of thinking that other people give a damn — but they really don't. I hate to break it to you, but sometimes even our own families and friends don't really give a damn about our businesses.

Many entrepreneurs make the mistake of thinking that people care about their product or service, or that all they have to do is put an ad in the Yellow Pages and say that they're in business at a certain location, and the people will come. But

> **Take good care of the people who take good care of you!**

remember, this is exactly what a good USP isn't. Most people won't spare something like this a second glance. It's not necessarily that they're lazy and apathetic; in most cases, they're just plain busy. On top of that, they're so bombarded with marketing that they usually don't have the time to think about or care about what they're hearing. If anything, they feel like they're overwhelmed with advertising messages.

If you can realize that most people not only don't give a damn about your advertising, your company, and what you're trying to sell them, but on the contrary, actually hate it — then you're of the proper mindset. Once you realize how fed up with advertising people are, you can start adjusting your message so it really does do all the great things I'm talking about here. Whatever it is you're selling, you have to get people to stop and pay attention — and that's what a USP is all about. If you can't get them to pay attention to you, they've got plenty of other things to do to keep themselves occupied.

Avoid Change for Change's Sake

If a USP just isn't working for you, don't hesitate to change it — but beware of changing a successful USP just because you've grown bored with it. This happens far more often than it should: marketing people get tired of the same old advertising, even though it works. **Somebody goes through a tremendous amount of time, money, and effort to develop a USP, to put together some great marketing campaigns, business just grows by leaps and bounds, and then they get bored and start**

changing everything.

A good example is the Schlitz story I mentioned earlier. Several years after Hopkin's innovative idea, some not-so-bright marketer said, "You know, we need a catchphrase for our Schlitz Beer," and they changed the whole marketing strategy to this: "Schlitz, the beer that made Milwaukee famous." And now Schlitz Beer is nowhere in the Top 10, or even Top 20, of all beer sold in America. In fact, the company barely exists as such, these days. This shows you how you can have the right USP, and how you can go back and change it and get the wrong one.

In advertising they have a saying: "By the time the client gets bored with the message and wants to change, it's probably making its first impression on the public." **Here's a word to the wise: get a good thing going and keep it going.** A great way to think of your marketing is to picture it as a parade. Your business is on a parade float, and at the beginning you're all excited about being on the float and you see the flowers, and the papier-mâché, and you're waving at the people and having a good time. Then, after about 30 minutes you're getting hot, and you realize that the papier-mâché is flaking off, and you're sweating and you hate it, and you want to jump off that float and get onto another. **What you don't realize is that the people the parade is passing by are seeing you for the first time.** They're excited. They're waving. Down the way a bit, there are even more people who've never seen you before, and they're excited to see you. Further on down, there are even more people happy to see you!

The long and the short of it is, most companies just get bored, because they see the same marketing every day. They want to jump off that float, even though it's still effective. "Oh, that slogan is so old. These sales letters are bad. Our USP is worn out; we've had it now for six months." So what? Some companies keep the same USP for years and years. Why would they do that? Because it continues to work. **Don't change your USP just because you're bored. If it's working, if it's making money — stick to it.**

In business, we tend to monkey with things more than we should, when if we'd let the customers continue to tell us what they want by studying their buying patterns, we'd be a lot better off. **If the USP stops working because sales are low, then by all means change it;** find a new USP, adjust it, tweak it, do whatever you need to. **But to change your USP just because you're tired of it or bored with it is a bad idea.** If the customers still like it and your sales are good, keep riding that baby as long as you can!

Summing It Up

As I wind down this chapter, I want to give you a quick recap of the things I've talked about here. In a way, these **concepts are entirely unfair to your competitors — because if you use them to create your USP, they'll separate you from every other competitor in your marketplace and let you dominate that marketplace.** But hey — there's a reason this is called the Ruthless Marketing System, right? You've got to be ruthless if you want to stay alive in our increasingly competitive marketplace.

Identify the Enemy

Take a look at the people who sell the exact same goods and services in your marketplace. **Who are your top five competitors, and why?** You've got to figure out what they're doing right, what they're doing wrong. What do they do to attract and retain the best customers and clients? You've got to spy on them, study them, become a customer. You've got to know them better than they know themselves. **You've got to know their strengths and weaknesses and try to focus in on those, because nobody makes money by accident.** If they're doing well consistently, they're doing something right.

Identify the Biggest Problems and Unfulfilled Needs in Your Market

What are the three biggest problems your prospects and customers face on a daily basis? What do your best prospects and customers want and need that they're not getting anywhere else? Answer these questions right, and you'll have a great USP. Build your Claims Matrix, so you can find where the gaps are. Where are the unfulfilled promises? Where are the biggest dissatisfactions? Work to create the great solutions to the biggest problems. To do this, you've got to brainstorm, brainstorm, and brainstorm!

> **A**ll growth comes from consciously living outside of your comfort zone. If you're not doing things on a regular basis that scare you just a little (or a lot!) — you're not growing.

Make Your Benefits Clear To Your Customers

Every USP requires a clear statement of benefits. Don't assume that your customers know what they'll get when they deal with you instead of Joe Blow down the street. Tell them exactly what you can do for them, and why they should come to you instead. If you've got the best-quality muffins in town, flaunt it. If your service is unique, take advantage of that. **People need**

to know how you're going to make their lives better.

Just Get Your USP Out There

I can't overstate the importance of formulating your USP and getting it out there where your clients can see it. It's too easy to get caught in the paralysis of analysis. You say to yourself, "It has to be perfect! I've got to get it just right!" Well, no, it doesn't. As I've made clear, you can refine your USP after you've launched it, as long as you don't overdo it. Don't think your USP has to be perfect right out of the box. As a small businessperson, you have the ability to be flexible. **If you can come up a great USP right now, and if down the road there's an ever better one and an even better advantage to your business, then you can change it.** Take a little bit of time and effort, get your USP out there and, believe me, even if it's not the best of the best of the best, you're going to be head and shoulders above the rest of your competitors.

Refine That USP

This one goes hand-in-glove with the previous point. **Once your USP's out there, you can refine it as needed.** Here are some good guidelines to follow: keep it short and clear. Keep it benefit-oriented. Make your claims believable. Make them measurable, if possible, as in time or quantity. Avoid defining your USP on price alone; someone can always beat you on that. **Make your claim unique, and use your proposition everywhere you can.**

That's a good place to end this chapter. I hope you understand a little better the fact that putting together a decent USP and making money with it really does take an intimate understanding of your best customers, their likes and dislikes, the challenges they face, the problems that keep them up at night, and the frustrations that they live with. The more you know about all of that, plus the more aware you are of those few competitors who are out there kicking butt in the marketplace, the better. Watch them closely. **Good companies are few and far between; that makes them easy to spot, if you know what to look for. Keep a close eye on them, and you'll find the right type of messages, through experimentation, because your customers will respond.** They'll respond with their checkbooks, their credit cards, and their cash.

4

Direct-Response Marketing

In this chapter, I'll introduce you to Direct-Response Marketing, and show you how you can use this powerful tool to dramatically increase your profits. The tips, tricks. and strategies I'll reveal to you here can make you huge sums of money, but you're going to have to read this chapter several times to really understand it. **Direct-Response Marketing is a complicated subject that deserves in-depth study.**

At its most basic, Direct-Response Marketing is whatever you do to get your customers to respond to you directly. It's not the kind of brand awareness you see when Pepsi or AT&T run a commercial on TV. That's not really asking you to do anything; it's just them getting their name out there. Direct-Response Marketing, on the other hand, is meant to get people to respond to you directly: to pick up the phone and call you, or to fill out an order form and fax it or mail it to you. **It's anything you do in business to get people to order from you, or to request more information, or to take a specific action.**

In some ways, I consider Direct-Response Marketing an art form. It's the process of identifying the audience most likely to purchase your product or service, and then approaching them directly at the right time to solicit their business, using a direct-to-consumer advertising medium. This can be postcards or other mailings, sales calls, special emails, handing out discount cards — **any form of advertising that directly targets potential and existing customers,** rather than something just thrown out there in hopes that someone will remember you when it comes time to fix the muffler or buy roses for Mother's Day. I call it an art form because it takes a while to understand and perfect the strategies you *must* use to truly match the right people with the right message at the right time.

But Direct-Response Marketing is also very much a science. It's an organized, multi-step system for selling, which starts off by targeting and contacting the people who might be interested in what you're selling, in such a way that you get them to respond and make their interest clear. Then the system kicks in, working to elicit their response again and get them more involved in what it is you're offering. This works whether you do it through direct mail, on the Internet, in seminars, or even one-on-one. **The science is also in the mechanics that make it all work: the ability to put together a database, to build a list, and to market to various elements of that list.** Regardless of the advertising media or strategies you choose, you have to immerse yourself in the science if you want to even get close to achieving art.

You have to employ the mechanics of Direct-Response Marketing in a way that makes sense to **the people you want to build relationships with**. You have to get their attention, you have to grab their interest, you have to create desire, and then you have to get them to take action. If you do that right, eventually you'll be able to create your masterpiece — the kind of life you want to live, lubricated by copious amounts of money.

The Name of the Game

Your goal with Direct-Response Marketing is to get an immediate action from your prospect, whether it's a visit

> The real business is between our ears and in our hearts — *not in the office!*

to your business, a call, an order, a purchase, a request for more information, or a promise. To accomplish any of these things, you need to create **salesmanship in print**. Not only does your Direct-Response Marketing strategy need to evoke an immediate action, but it also has to do everything a real salesman would do, in terms of generating that response. **Just like a living, breathing salesman, here's what that a good Direct-Response Marketing campaign does**:

- It tells the prospect about the benefits of the product;

- It overcomes objection;

- It answers questions;

- It provides a guarantee; and

- It makes promises.

A good Direct-Response Marketing campaign does all these things and more; it has to, in order to succeed. I think the biggest benefit of Direct-Response Marketing over face-to-face salesmanship or even telemarketing is that you have the power to let Yellow Page ads, sales letters, classified ads, or display ads in the newspaper, magazines or on the Internet generate the response you're looking for. Direct-Response Marketing allows you to multiply your effort, to reach a lot more people, and generate a lot more responses without wasting your time — and that makes it a very powerful strategy indeed.

In order to work effectively, Direct-Response Marketing has to be a very targeted form of marketing. Think of a rifle, versus a shotgun. With Direct-Response Marketing, you don't just blast out a message to everyone at random: **your message is delivered in the clearest and most compelling way possible, to the specific people who are most likely to buy and then continue to buy from you.** Those people could be highly qualified prospects that you've identify through various methods, or they can be established customers, people with whom you already have an ongoing relationship.

Marketers use lots of metaphors to describe Direct-Response Marketing. In addition to being a combination of art and science, to many of us it's also a combination of sport and war. This is a fun way of making money. You can be very strategic using this marketing method, just as a couple of generals would be when planning how to stage an attack on their enemy. Because make no mistake: no matter how much you'd like to believe otherwise, **your direct competitors are your enemies**. They're out there trying to get the same dollars you're trying to get, and you can't let that happen.

Laying a Firm Foundation

Direct Marketing is a system for selling, and if **you don't have a system for selling, then you're at the mercy of your customer's system for buying — and they don't have one.** What most businesses do — sadly for them, but fortunately for you — is the direct opposite of Direct-Response Marketing.

They set up shop, put up some signs, and maybe run the occasional radio ad or newspaper spot, but they do it in such a way that it's mildly effective at best. They're not using Direct-Response Marketing to get people into their selling system.

Now, in order to do Direct-Response Marketing right, you need to start with a firm foundation. One excellent way to do this is to achieve an intimate understanding of what I call the *Three Keys to Effective Direct-Response Marketing*. These keys will help you do Direct-Response Marketing right; I've seen a lot of people make a lot of mistakes that could easily have been avoided if they'd just done the simple things I'm going to tell you to do here. The Three Keys are relatively straightforward, and they strip Direct-Response Marketing down to its basic elements. Without further ado, here's what you have to have to do effective Direct-Response Marketing:

- The right message
- The right audience
- The right time

Or to put it all together into one sentence, **you've got to carry the right message to the right audience at the right time.** I consider this the Golden Rule of Direct-Response Marketing.

Many marketers boil this concept down to what they call the KISS Principle, where KISS stands for "Keep It Simple, Stupid." I think that's a little offensive, so I'll use my own term, thank you. Now, if you don't get the right message to the right audience at the right time, you're going to hear "no" a lot more than you'll hear "yes." **Instead of using a shotgun, pull up that high-powered rifle, identify exactly who the prospect is who's most**

likely to buy your product, and go directly to that consumer using a direct-to-consumer advertising medium. In the following sections, I'm going to discuss all these things in greater detail, and in the order I think is most important.

Key One: The Audience

If you don't play to the right audience, you're never going to have a very good response to anything you do. You've failed right from the beginning: game over, time to go home. Identifying the right people is the most important key to successful Direct-Response Marketing, and I suggest you use three methods to accomplish this.

Human beings love to repeat the same behaviors over and over again. If you can get them to do something one time — you can get them to do it the next time.

First is what I call "customer hijacking" — or **letting your competition do your work for you.** This is simply where you go out and rent a list of your competition's customers and then try to make them your own. It's not possible for every industry, but it's the number one tactic I suggest *if* it's possible. So if you're Sears, and J. C. Penney is selling appliances, you try to get a list of those people they've recently sold appliances to. Then you can send them a Direct Mail piece that gives them the option of buying their next appliance from you.

Second is demographic profiling: analyzing your target audience and **coming up with the profile of your ultimate customer or target audience.** In using demographics like age, gender, income level, and location, you're basically looking for anything that helps you identify who's most likely to buy your products and services. Once you've figured that out, you can go out and acquire a list of clients who meet those criteria. You're going to use list brokers for both customer hijacking and demographic profiling.

Third is customer corralling. This is where you capture information on your past or current customers, and add them to a list so you can continue to solicit business. Keep in mind that **the easiest sale you're ever going to make is to a customer to whom you've already sold.** A good example of this is Harrah Casinos' Loyalty Programs. You go in there to gamble one time, they get you on a little card, and pretty soon you're getting more mail than you've ever known — and you're going back to Harrah's a lot more often.

Key Two: Your Message

Now, let's talk about the right message. You need to **study your products or services from your customer's perspective.** Remember, it's all about them; you have to keep in mind their view, which can be summarized as WIIFM — *What's In It For Me?* That's what your prospects want to know. So build your message around the strongest benefits to your customer, and keep in mind that there are only five real reasons people buy anything: greed, guilt, fear, pride, or love. We marketers call this the *psychographic* of your audience, as opposed to the demographic; and **the two most important of those psychographic motives are greed and fear.** That's why you see so many commercials that play on people's greed, or that make them afraid that they're doing something wrong: raising their children wrong, not brushing their teeth enough, or not wearing the right deodorant.

You need to **understand the emotional reasons that**

---

people buy products and services. Make sure you build your benefits toward one or more of those reasons. Identify your customer's strongest motives to buy, and you're going to do very well identifying the right message.

Key Three: the Right Time

Once you've identified the right audience and the right message, **you need to identify the time your prospects are most likely to purchase your product or service.** For example, if you run a mortgage company, aim your message at people who are selling their houses. If a person's selling a house, they'll most likely need to buy a new house shortly thereafter — so if you hit them with a mortgage opportunity right then and there, there's a good chance they'll take it. If you wait three weeks or a month after your prospect puts his property on the market, chances are that he's already found another mortgage if he was planning to buy another piece of property. Therefore, you need to respond within a few days, no more. If you plan this properly and do it correctly, the time *will* be right.

Effective Direct-Response Marketing is all about the right audience, the right message, and the right timing. And while I've discussed Direct-Response Marketing as an art form, don't worry about going out there and trying to paint the *Mona Lisa* right off the bat. **It's kind of like playing chess. You might start out a bit slow, but you're going to get better at it the more you do it.** Like chess, Direct-Response Marketing takes a day to learn and a lifetime to master; but use these guidelines, and you'll have a solid foundation to build your business on.

What Kind of Bait's on Your Hook?

One thing you should be aware of from the get-go is that **Direct-Response Marketing isn't cheap.** If you use it right you can make millions, but as the old saying goes, it takes money to make money. Continuing with the mortgage example, here's an interesting way that some people have attracted new customers. They combine the right message with the right audience at the right time, they send their message by Federal Express — already an expensive proposition — and then they sweeten the proposition by throwing a $100 bill in that Federal Express package. That's right — a $100 bill. You see, they know it's a numbers game, but it's also a game of finding the right people to deliver your message to, and knowing that **you can spend a lot more money to reach that right person** (assuming that other things — your price points and your profit margins — are high).

> **T**RUE POWER IS KNOWING YOUR STRENGTHS AND WEAKNESSES. Don't lie to yourself about these two areas. Most people tend to overestimate their chances of success and underestimate their chances of failure. You must become stronger in the areas you are already strong in and delegate (not abdicate) your weakest areas.

So these marketers are throwing a $100 bill in a Federal Express envelope, and then sending a personalized letter along with it. There's none of that "Dear Friend" crap — that's counterproductive. Instead, they're saying, "Dear John: Why have I sent you a $100 bill by Federal Express? Two reasons: **1)** Your time is very valuable, so I'm paying you well to spend a good, solid hour looking over everything in this package; and **2)** I believe you're the type of person I'm looking for, and I'm willing to back up my beliefs with a solid investment." That's an excellent example of getting the right message to the right prospect at the right time, and not being afraid to spend a lot of money in the process.

So many people fail with Direct-Response Marketing, and they don't have to. This is a $300 billion a year industry; so why doesn't it work for them? When you dig a little deeper, it turns out that **they didn't have their hearts in it**. They sent out some postcards, they didn't get the results they expected, and they gave up. They thought they were doing Direct-Response Marketing — but they're really weren't. *You have to spend money with Direct-Response Marketing to make money.* It could be worth it to send out $100 bills once you know what your customers are worth. You want to get their attention, and their time is valuable, and paying them for it is a great way to grab them by the throat and make them give you a fair hearing.

P. T. Barnum, who is one of my heroes — a great, great marketer — once said, "Don't try to catch a whale by using a minnow as bait. **"If there's one general mistake I see a lot, one that people who are brand new to Direct-Response Marketing are making over and over, it's that they want huge results from the very beginning**. They're expecting enormous things from this form of marketing, which it can and does deliver to the people who understand how to use it. But they're starting out trying to capture a whale by using a minnow as bait, and in doing so they're being *far* too conservative. **As long as you've found the right customer and the right message, and the rest of your mechanics are in place, you can afford to spend a ton of money to reach that person."**

If I said this approach always works, I'd be lying. You don't know for sure what's going to happen. Even if it's the right thing to do, you're going to reach a certain percentage of people who can't follow through because other things are going on in their lives. Maybe, for example, they've just broken their leg, or they're getting a divorce, or they've lost their job. So you won't catch every prospect, but remember: you won't catch any if you use the wrong bait. Don't be afraid to gamble a little, because if you're trying to catch a whale by using a minnow as bait, you'll never have any real success.

Knowing What You're Doing

Here's another thing I'd like to add about the person who says, "Well, I sent out a postcard one time and I didn't get any responses." When I hear that, I say, "Let me see your sales material." Usually, I find that they've done a terrible job of getting their message across. Sometimes people believe they're great writers, and they're not; or they're not focusing on right kind of communication. They may write copy that sounds really good and has a lot of big words in it, and what those big words do to a lot of people is turn them off. Many of their readers might not understand them, and **a confused mind says "no" automatically.** Also, if a prospect doesn't understand a word, they may subconsciously feel like they're stupid. They shut off at that point.

There are all kinds of factors that go into Direct-Response Marketing that a novice isn't even aware of. They may have written a postcard, and had their buddy with an English degree edit it so it's grammatically correct and looks nice, but it just doesn't elicit the response they wanted — because they didn't really know what they wanted it to do, or they didn't know how to compel people to say "yes." **In order to solicit business, you need to get into those psychographic factors I mentioned before (fear, greed, guilt, love, and pride), as well as the nuts-and-bolts science of what makes people say yes.**

If you don't know how to do this, don't try to wing it: either hire people who do, or go find people who've done it and emulate them. Don't steal from them, but model your copy after what they've done. **Do the things you know have already been successful for others, then fine-tune those strategies so they can work for you.** There are a lot of strategies floating around out there, and lots of little ways to tweak your performance. Even the colors of your postcards can make a difference in response. As a Direct Response Marketer, you're going to have to do a lot of things you've never done before. Think of all these things as broadening your education.

> We are all self-made… but only the successful will admit it.

You'll want to continue to market to your prospects in a systemized manner, using follow-up campaign sequences — one following the other. This will cost you some money, but it's justified. Once you implement the three keys I talked about earlier —getting the right message to the right people at the right time — you're not done. That's really where you start. Do those things right, and you're going to grab a nice percentage of your target audience; they'll go through your selling process, and you'll make some money. But you need to continue to market to them! Once you've gotten the responses from a mailing, do a second mailing, and then another. **The great thing about Direct-Response Marketing is that you know the results very quickly** — with direct mail, for example, it may take a couple of weeks, at most. Online it's even faster.

Once again, remember this: your offer does need to be tweaked and made more efficient, but it doesn't have to be a masterpiece from the word go; it just has to be good enough. Once you've got everything together and you've followed all the steps, go for it. Send it out, and learn from what happens. You don't have to flood the market right away, either — you can test and improve on your message quickly if you **start out slowly**. Start mailing, testing, sending out little bits and pieces, and see what happens.

AIDA Ain't Just an Opera

Here's an interesting acronym that some of my fellow marketers find useful: AIDA. It stands for:

- **A**ttention
- **I**nterest
- **D**esire
- **A**ction

AIDA dovetails nicely with the three keys we've already discussed here. But these four elements have more to do with the overall process once you've already targeted your prospects and figured out what you want to say, and you know you have the timing down.

Once you've done all these things, look at the actual Direct Marketing media available: the piece, the letter, the ad, the email message, or whatever it is. **First of all, you need to grab your prospect's Attention**, and typically you're going to do that with your headline. That's what it'll be in print or on a website; if it's an email, it's your subject. If you're addressing people in a conference, it's the first thing you say. If it's a postcard, it's in bold print. The headline has to grab their attention and make them want to read further. That's its only purpose — to grab their attention, and get them interested in continuing to read.

One of the greatest headlines ever was Dale Carnegie's "How To Win Friends and Influence People." "How to" headlines are not only often the easiest to come up with — because you already have the first two words down — but quite often they're also the most effective. What should that "how to" promise? **It needs to be benefit-laden.** I've mentioned "What's In It For Me?" already. WIIFM is the essence of writing your headline.

Once you get their attention, you need to grab their Interest. Quite often, this is done with a sub-headline that states your Unique Selling Proposition. It answers the question in the prospect's mind: "Why should I deal with this person or company, or buy this service, or get involved in this, or even accept this free report over all the others out there?"

Your next goal is to stimulate a Desire as they get into your offer. Most people think in words, but they take those words and put them into pictures. A picture is a stronger, more effective way of thinking. Most people, being visual, require the painting of these word pictures in their minds, and that's what you want to do as you tell your story. You want them to be in this story; they're the star of the show you're creating here. That's how you really create desire in people: by the way you place them in the copy, and the way you overcome their initial apprehension. Testimonials from people who have benefited from what you offer can work wonders here.

Now we come to the second "A," which is **Action. You have to make sure that it's easy and convenient for prospects to become customers.** This is where you ask for their response, whether it's an order, or for them to call an 800 number, or to send an email — whatever it is you want them to do. This is where you make it convenient for them to respond. Give your prospects several ways to get in touch with you. You don't want to give them too many choices, ever, on anything, but you want to give them basic choices. This is where understanding your customer is really important. Some people may have misgivings about certain ways of responding to you, so you want to give them options that are comfortable for them. Maybe the psychodemographics of your customer base makes them more likely to pick up the phone and call a number; or maybe they'd prefer to fax their order in. You should also give them the option to mail their order in, even if you're strictly doing an online transaction. That's a big mistake I often see online: not even offering that option. The way a lot of websites work — you put your credit card in or you don't buy, and that's a mistake. Some people just don't feel safe putting their credit card number out there in cyberspace.

Calls to Action

Let's go back to something I touched on earlier: the way that **many businesses try Direct-Response Marketing, then dump it quickly because it doesn't work for them.** That's because they're not using it right. I've discussed using the right bait, and this next point plays into that concept: you have to give your customers a great offer. Some businesses try Val-Pak, where you get all these little full-color inserts about various businesses; you've probably gotten these packets yourself. But that's not Direct-Response Marketing. That's just coupon marketing. Most of the coupons are horrible because they're either designed by the advertiser, who doesn't know how to market properly, or they're designed by a person who wants to get the work done and move on to the next customer. Yes, you're sending that coupon

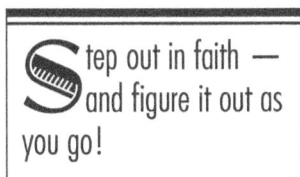

> **S**tep out in faith — and figure it out as you go!

out to a list of human beings, but it's not targeted, and the ads are uninspired. If you look at them, basically what they're saying is, "Hey, we're your plumber! We've been in business for 80 years. We're the best in the business!" That's not Direct-Response Marketing, because that doesn't evoke an action. Someone who gets that will say, "Wow, they've been in business 80 years. I'd go crazy if I had to do plumbing for 80 years! Poor suckers!" And then they throw it away.

You have to give people an offer that will evoke an action. Maybe you've done some image advertising, where you just try to get your name out in front of people, say through postcards or in the Yellow Pages, and hope that somebody will contact you because your ad just happened to appear when they had a plumbing problem, or they needed an attorney, or whatever your business is — but that's not going to happen very often. You absolutely have to target your market, you have to get the right message to them, and you have to use the right timing. **You need to capture their attention by making them an offer that will actually get them to take an action — whether that's calling your business, coming by, or purchasing something from you.**

One great example is a gentleman by the name of Bob Stupak, the founder of the Stratosphere Casino in Las Vegas. As you know, most Las Vegas casinos do image advertising. They don't say, "Come on in, we've got this special deal for you," and things like that; instead, they've got these beautiful billboards and beautiful ads, and they show the fountains out in front and the people gambling and having fun inside. That's supposed to be enough to evoke an action in you, to have you come to their casino. Well, Bob Stupak was a great marketer as well as a great gambler. **When he started out, the Stratosphere was a tiny casino, and he needed to pull people in, so he created an**

offer: for $198 you got a three-day, two-night stay at his casino. You paid this in advance, before you ever showed up, and you had an entire year to use it. He ran his ads in *Parade* magazine and did Direct Mail and got his ads out everywhere. It wasn't an image ad; it was an actual *offer*. For $198 you got a three-day, two-night stay at the casino, but you also got two tickets to their headliner show, several meal coupons, as much as $500 in slot tokens, and $200 in casino chips.

People bought into Stupak's offer like crazy. He was selling literally tens of thousands of these packages, and that's how **he built the Stratosphere into a multi-billion dollar business.** It was a hot offer, and he continued to make it better and throw in more bonuses over time. Here's the kicker: plenty of people bought the offer, but only a relatively small percentage ever actually showed up at his casino. So all those people who didn't show up, didn't take up space in the room, didn't come to get their chips — they'd still paid all that money, and he got to pocket that.

Now you're thinking, "Okay, that's a casino. How am I going to make a hot offer like that to my customers?" **Use your imagination. There are people in every business niche — plumbers, attorneys, restaurateurs — who are making hot offers people can't turn down.** There aren't very many of them, but they're out there. Here's another example: there's a certain restaurateur who realized early on that the lifetime value of each of his customers was very high. He knew that if he could get people into his restaurant to sit down and eat a meal, they'd come back not one or two times, but five times, 20 times, 100 times. They'd be coming back for many years, which made the lifetime value of the typical customer literally thousands of dollars.

So, what was his offer? He mailed out sales letters to people in his area, and offered them a free meal. That's right. I'm not talking about a "buy one, get one free" deal, or a child's meal free if you bought an adult meal. There were no strings attached: he offered an actual free meal. You got the entrée, you got an appetizer, you got your drink. Every single thing was free! In his sales letter, he told the truth about why he wanted you to come in and enjoy this free meal: it was because he knew you would come back again and again, since the food was so great. **His business practically exploded, because people thought that was an incredible deal.** They'd come in, enjoy the meal, and then come back again and again.

This takes us back to the concept of how much money you're willing to spend to get people into your business. A lot of business people are scared to go too far out on a limb; they don't want to spend too much of their limited advertising budget. Maybe a few cents for postage on a postcard is all they think they can afford. **But if you're delivering the services people want, and you're giving great value, and you have customers with a very high lifetime value, you can afford to make great offers in order to get prospects in the door.** You can go negative on that initial offer and still make money.

> **People want to do business with people just like them**

Your offer doesn't even have to be a price deal. Let's say you're stuck on your price: maybe you can't give your customers the lowest price out there, or maybe you don't even want to try. Instead, give more for what you're selling. For example, let's say you're a dentist. You can offer a lot more things than just a regular cleaning. You might say, "Come in, and we're going to give you a regular cleaning and a personalized toothbrush. Then we're going to have a customer appreciation party, and every six months you can get a free ticket for yourself and your family. We've got free drinks and free food." You can throw anything in there! **There's all sorts of crazy stuff you can do to create a great offer that catches prospects and brings them in.** If you make good on your promises, you're going to keep them.

So get over your fear of trying something wild to draw your customers in. The response can be phenomenal. Make a tremendous offer; do things that shock people; do things that would scare most business owners to death. Now, you don't have to be a fool about it. **One of the greatest things about Direct-Response Marketing is that you can test all kinds of wild and crazy and outrageous ideas to a small group of customers, so you're not really risking a lot of money if it doesn't work.** You can make sure you take what we call a stratified sample of your list and market to that — assuming you've built up a list.

You can stratify or segment your list by the products and services your customers buy, or by the dollar amount they spend, or by the last time they did business with you. The reason you do this is because, first of all, you can tell everything about a person from their actions. When somebody's buying a certain type of product or service from you, that speaks volumes. Or, if you have a few customers who are spending ten times more money than the rest of your customers, those people are showing, by the money they spend, a certain level of seriousness that the rest of your customers aren't showing. **You've got to be able to segment those smaller groups of better customers or to segment for other reasons so that you can speak directly to those groups of people in a different way than you speak to the rest of your customer list.**

So don't drop a Direct Mail campaign to your entire customer list with some crazy new idea that you're not sure is going to work. You want to see how a stratified sample is going to respond before you stretch your neck out too far. **Take little pockets of customers from your customer base and use them to test your wild and crazy stuff,** so you don't end up with a fiasco where everybody wants what you're offering, and you can't supply it to them all.

This brings up another point. When you're building your offer, you can also add a line like this one: "While supplies last." This will invoke urgency in your prospects, because now they know they'll need to hurry to get all the extra things you're throwing into your offer. In addition, this covers your bases in case you get an overzealous response. Your prospects won't mind being part of a small, select group, because when you market to a stratified sample, you're actually treating those customers special. Go ahead and tell them what you're doing; they'll appreciate being treated special. And to you, they *should* be special, because by marketing to them first, you're lowering your overall risk.

Common Sense — It's So Uncommon

It's easy to wonder why more people don't try test-marketing offers the way I've outlined above. I think one of the big reasons they don't do it is that they don't know *how* to do it. **Most people learn marketing by looking at other marketers in their field.** So if their major competitor is running a half-page Yellow Pages ad, they think they'd better do that — instead of thinking, "Okay, maybe this isn't the right way to do it." Well, sometimes in marketing **you have to go against the flow, and**

do something that makes you stand head and shoulders above the crowd. Then, once you know that, you have to get past the fear. If you own a restaurant, you may be thinking: "Good Lord, I can't even imagine giving away a free meal. I've got staff, I've got food costs, and I've got overhead. I can't even imagine making that type of a deal." You've got to break through that fear barrier.

So once you've got your offer, **test it to a small portion of your list, and see what happens.** You don't have to mail it out to 20,000 people in your area; you can mail it out to a couple of hundred people and see what the response is. If it does well, roll it out to more people. **If it doesn't do well, try something else.** It's important to at least make that offer. Because if you don't, you're going to continue to market like everybody else and continue to get the same type of response as everybody else — and in most cases, that's a pretty poor response.

> When asking, ASK BOLDLY.

If you don't already have a list, you need to build one. A lot of businesses are of the opinion that they don't need one: "I don't have a list. People come in, they buy, they leave." But not creating a list that they can use for Direct-Response Marketing is where a lot of people stumble. **There's gold in your customer list, because you're able to go back to those people, make more offers, and get them back into your business — as opposed to always going out and trying to bring brand new people in, hoping that the people who did business with you one time will remember you the second time.** If you're hoping, instead of actually mailing to a list that you've created, you're not going to be making as much money as if you were smart enough to get some simple database software, ask people for

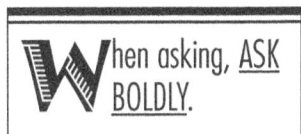

their names and contact information, and actually mail to the resulting list.

Most merchants aren't even gathering up their customers' names to begin with —and frankly, that's just ridiculous. **If you ask most business owners how much money they spend on communicating and building relationships with their existing customers, most would say, "Huh?" They may spend money to** *attract* **new customers, and they think that's what advertising and marketing is. Real marketing, however, is customer relationship marketing** — and that's now an accepted way of running a business, thanks to a lot of us Direct-Response Marketers who've proven that it's successful to build and maintain those relationships. It makes sense, but so many businesses out there just don't grasp it, and they don't spend a dime to develop and maintain relationships with their customers.

Then again, **you could just do like just about everyone else, and sit around and wait for customers to come to you.** Let me share with you a story I heard from my good friend Russ von Hoelscher. He knows a guy who has a print shop in a little strip mall, and the guy's always whining and complaining about how bad business is. Russ likes the guy, but he gets sick and tired of hearing him moan. So one day Russ said, "Look, John, there's got to be 400 businesses within a five-mile radius of here. Since you've got those printing presses, why don't you just print up some sales material and I'll help you, and we can target all those businesses, and you can get them to start coming to you." And here's what the guy said to Russ: "People want printing, they can come to me." That was his whole attitude! It's ignorant, it's horrible, and it's unbelievable. Apparently, **it's easier to whine and cry and complain about how bad things are than to do a thing to change it.** Unfortunately, that mindset is more common that you might think.

It's Two, Two, Two Mints in One!

In the introduction to this chapter, I pointed out that Direct-Response Marketing is often considered both an art and as science, and I want to focus on that perception in this section. I want to clarify the fact that there's absolutely no way to achieve art, or even get close to it, without understanding the science involved in Direct-Response Marketing — and it's immense. So how are you going to master such a big topic, with all the variables it includes? You can start by breaking it down: learn the technology that's used to reach your market, for starters. If you're using a specific medium, you've got to understand how the process works, how to get the best rates, and what resources you have at your disposal to let you best use this medium, whether it's TV, radio, the Internet, or print. Knowing the technology used to reach your market is one key to your success, and it's all part of the science.

Another part is database management. Building or finding a list of highly qualified prospects is key. Knowing and tracking your market is also crucial. You need to know what they've purchased in the past and why they bought what they bought, because this will help you to sell them in the future.

Something I've mentioned several **times is understanding the psychological aspects of marketing — the emotional factors that prompt people to buy or to act.** Those are, again, pride, love, fear, greed, and guilt. **Practice weaving those psycho-logical factors into your copy, into your message, into your headlines, and into your sub-headlines, because that will ultimately produce the actions you're wanting.** Now, you just can't say to yourself, "Okay, I'm going to really concentrate on pride," and whip out something that sucks in the customers. **It takes practice. It takes time to understand your style, and how you're going to invoke these factors in your audience.**

Another important factor here is communication:

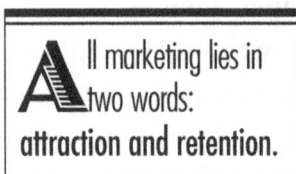

> **A**ll marketing lies in two words: **attraction and retention.**

learning to use plain, direct, and simple words and ideas, because a confused mind says "no." If you're writing something and you think, "Man, that's really clever, the way I did that," then you might be overthinking things. There's no need to be cute with this type of writing. You want to grab them by the heart or grab them by the gonads or grab them by the mind, and the best way to do that is to do it with plain, direct speech.

Here's another big factor: **testing.** Yes, I'm repeating this too, because I want to make you see how important it is. **You don't want to commit tons of money to something you're not even the least bit sure is going to work.** Our example is the guy who tried a bunch of postcards and failed; we've talked a lot about him. He went out there, spent a lot of money on getting them printed up and on the postage to send them out — and it flopped dead. Well, that money is just gone, because he didn't test his postcard before he sent it out. He wasted his advertising dollars.

As I mentioned at the start of this section, **there's no way to achieve art without understanding the science.** It's like when you first learned to ride a bike and you had training wheels, and it was fun. You learned that you pedaled and it made you go, and you learned how the brakes worked. But then you took those training wheels off, and pretty soon you were building ramps so you could jump your bike and do crazy stunts. The same thing goes with immersing yourself in the science of Direct-Response Marketing. You learn how it works, you learn the ins and outs and how to do it cost-effectively, and next thing you know you're jumping from ramp to ramp and you're building success on success. **The art simply won't come unless you understand the science. The science allows you to know your audience, know where to find them, know what to say, and know how to say it.**

You may never get to where Direct-Response Marketing is an art form for you, but that's a goal you can set for yourself — and maybe, someday, you'll end up painting the ceiling of the Sistine Chapel. You're always striving for that masterpiece. I've already told you that **marketing is something that takes a day to learn and a lifetime to master. The real art comes only after a lot of work.** It's no accident that the best freelance Direct Response Marketers are charging thousands of dollars for every piece they write, plus a nice chunk of the residual royalty income from the gross sales. These people have one thing in common: they've been doing it for a couple decades. There are some exceptions, but they're rare. The people in this world who are the best at this form of marketing, who really know how to do this, have been doing it for a long time.

Good Enough for Government Work

You're not going to create a perfect Direct-Response Marketing campaign from the start, but that shouldn't discourage you from trying. Remember, good enough is good enough, especially when you're starting out. You don't necessarily have to become an expert marketer before you take the plunge. The truth is, **some of the best marketing I've ever seen wasn't written by professionals — it was written by sincere business** people who really love what they're doing, who really want to connect with the prospect, and who don't know all the fancy tricks and marketing secrets that somebody who's been in the business 20 years might know. What they do have is *heart*. They have an understanding of a few of the basic principles, an understanding that you have to make an offer and you have to go to the right market with the right message at the right time. Knowing that, they're able to go out with a message that really hits home and drives business in.

Most people are convinced that advertising is best done by experts. The advertising agencies of the world want to convince you that all this is so damn complicated that you've got to be educated to do all this stuff. One of the definitions of Direct-Response Marketing I mentioned at the beginning of this chapter is that **Direct-Response Marketing is salesmanship in print.** I promise you, **the best salespeople aren't the ones who went to college and got a degree (with some very notable exceptions, of course). The best salespeople are the ones out there in the trenches, face-to-face, belly-to-belly, eyeball-to-eyeball with their best customers.** They've got relationships with those people. They know what those people want. They know how to give them what they want. They're out there serving them like crazy. Oftentimes the best Direct-Response Marketing doesn't look pretty; some of it really looks like crap! But it does a powerful job of getting the right message to the right customer at the right time. **It's just salesmanship: one person wanting to do business with another person.** Those are the people you want to emulate — the ones who are getting the job done, actually seeing results and generating a profit.

You're going to get better over time. Even better, once you've got it down, it's a skill you'll have forever. You're not relying on another company to create turnkey materials for you, take your money, and disappear. **You're able to create and make offers whenever you want, and that's a real power — a power to generate cash whenever you need it.** In that way, Direct-Response Marketing is the power to create money on demand. It's the opposite of just sitting around waiting for customers to come to you, which is what most people do. **Good marketers are proactive: they're out there attracting people.** They're not pushing; they're *pulling* people in with their messages. You can become one of those effective marketers. Once again, you don't really have to be perfect at it when you start out — it's actually quite a forgiving business. **You can make a ton of mistakes and still make a ton of money.**

Don't Overthink It

As human beings, we tend to overcomplicate things — and here's a good example. When NASA decided to send astronauts into space, on the first mission they discovered that the

> **M**arketing is simply a combination of <u>math</u> and <u>psychology</u>. — *Dan Kennedy*

common ballpoint pen wouldn't work in zero gravity. So they spent millions of dollars developing a pen that would write in outer space. Now they've got one that writes underwater, upside-down, in temperatures over 100 degrees, on ice-capped mountains — in just about any condition that anyone could possibly imagine. But the Russians did something else that was pretty elegant: they used pencils instead.

There's a tendency, when you're coming up with all these ideas and strategies, to get a little overwhelmed. But **there's no need to make your marketing more complicated than it has to be. Don't try to do everything at once. You can learn one**

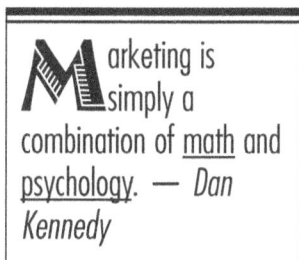

strategy and implement that strategy, then learn something else. Look at what other people do, then tweak and fine-tune your strategy at the level you're currently at. You don't have to do everything with every promotion. There are so many different elegant, simple ways to make money in Direct-Response Marketing.

Why Don't More People Do Direct-Response Marketing?

Most business owners don't do more Direct-Response Marketing because they don't understand it, and they don't realize it's one of the most cost-effective ways of advertising. They've been duped into thinking that other types of ads work better. Radio and television is what a lot of local businesses specifically focus their dollars on, at least in the very beginning — because it's a new business, the medium is glamorous, and they need new customers. Those media are actually training those advertisers to buy in that manner, and so advertisers often don't have the time to even consider Direct-Response Marketing.

And, of course, **there's hardly anybody showing up at their door to sell them good Direct-Response Marketing.** You've got the Yellow Page guy, who keeps bugging you to get a bigger ad. You've got the advertising specialty people, who want you to print up everything with your name on it. The newspapers and some radio and TV stations — those guys bug the hell out of you. But you don't have anybody coming along saying, "Look, I specialize in good Direct-Response Marketing that's relationship-building and long-term, using strategies that will let you quadruple your profits — or, in some cases, make more than ten of your competitors combined." There's nobody out there who's doing that as a profession.

A Dearth of Decent Offers

Here's one reason a lot of people don't do Direct-Response Marketing: they don't know how to define and create decent offers. They're simply buying the advertising they can afford, when they can afford it. Most advertisers think that Direct-Response Marketing has to be very expensive. Sure, you've got to cut through all the radio, TV, newspaper, and magazines ads, and all the crap your prospects are getting in their mail and on the Internet. Does that mean it has to cost a lot of money? No. You can give something away that has a large perceived value, but may not cost that much. It depends on exactly what your prospect wants.

Sadly, many advertisers don't even know what a decent offer *is*. I'll give you a good definition: **an offer is a reason to buy. It can be anything: a low price, unusual products, a special sale, special bonuses and extras — all the things you're offering to the customer in exchange for the money you want them to give to you.** Too much of the advertising out there doesn't have any real offer attached. People are spending their good, hard-earned dollars running this advertising — and they're not really trying to *sell* anything. They're not giving their prospects a clear and compelling reason to come do business with them right now.

In creating an offer, you should ask yourself what the prospect wants. If you're a restaurant owner, what do they want when they come into your restaurant? Let's say, for example, that you want to make a special offer for Valentine's Day, and normally you'd do "two-for-one," or you'd offer a free dessert, or something like that. Those aren't really eye-popping offers. Instead, think deeply about what your customers *really* want on

Valentine's Day. They want the whole romantic feel, right? So how about this: you offer a "Valentine's Day Lovers Package." If they come in as a couple, the female of the party is going to get a bunch of roses, and there's going to be free champagne and there's going to be chocolate-dipped strawberries. There's going to be a person going around playing romantic music on the violin. By creating that type of special offer, you're going to set yourself apart from all the other restaurants out there who want that Valentine's Day business. And as I mentioned before, make it a limited offer. Say something like, "There's a limited number of spaces so you'd better act fast, because these Valentine's Day packages will go quickly."

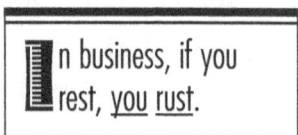

> In business, if you rest, you rust.

Here's a good idea that my colleague Randy Charach told me about. He was going to the same hairstylist quite often, and one day he noticed that she had a little sign hidden behind her box of scissors and some business cards that said, "Please refer me." She asked him, "You're the marketing expert. How can I get more business?" He said, "It's really simple. You can make yourself as busy as you want by doing what I'm going to tell you right now. I hope you do this, because I know it will work. Give out a card to every one of your customers that gives a free haircut, on the first visit, to anybody they give that card to. All you're doing is giving a free haircut once to one person."

Now, that's going to attract a lot of people to come for a free haircut. She does a good job, her price is reasonable, she's nice to talk to, and there's no reason for them not to come back. The only reason they may not even take her up this offer is that they're afraid to leave whomever they currently go to. That isn't the case with most people.

See? You don't have to spend much money to get good results from Direct-Response Marketing. If you can spend money, that's fine — maybe it's more profitable for you to do that. **You can afford to sell something for $50 that cost you $70, if you know the lifetime value of your customer is $1,000.** You've just got to do the numbers. **Direct Marketing is psychology and math, that's all it is:** figuring out what the people want and then calculating the metric. Most advertisers don't bother, just as they don't bother to build a decent customer list.

Summing It Up

There's a lot of money out there that's just lying on the table — and it's waiting for you to pick it up. This chapter shows you the tip of the iceberg regarding what Direct-Response Marketing can do for you. So let this be something that whets your appetite, and gets you hungry for more. Be sure you come back to this chapter and read it again. **Do everything possible to learn everything you can about Direct-Response Marketing, because it's something that can increase your profits dramatically and give you an unfair advantage in your marketplace.**

5

Front-End and Back-End Marketing Systems

In this chapter, I'm going to discuss front-end and back-end marketing systems, and why it's imperative that you develop your own. These systems are extremely important to any business, and if you'll practice the things I'm going to teach you here, you'll benefit dramatically.

Put simply, **front-end and back-end systems are the methods you use to attract customers, and then to sell to them again later.** I look at front-end sales as low-cost hand-raisers that you use as an introduction to new prospects, so they can express an interest in what you have to sell. **But every front-end system is created and offered with the intention of making a back-end sale of a much higher-priced item.** Your front-end breaks the ice; it's the secret to breaking through your inability to sell high-ticket items to people who don't know you. It lets you make that initial introduction, and identify those who are interested in what you've got to offer.

You should look at your sales system as a funnel. You're trying to bring in a large number of would-be buyers and get them into that huge opening at the top. **You use a low-cost (or even a *no*-cost) offer to do this, but only to get them acquainted with you and what you have to offer. The back-end is where you really make your money.** Once you've broken the ice, most of your would-be customers will fall by the wayside; and that's okay, because **you're looking for the wheat, not the chaff.** You simply have to take in a huge amount of people to get that small percentage of customers who will buy in the back-end, and then continue to buy from you in the future.

What it all boils down to is this: **the front-end sale — that first sale at the top of the funnel — is meant to get a prospect on your buyers list.** That's all it's for; it's not about profit, although it's nice if you can make a little. This is where a lot of people make their biggest mistake: they think that the front-end sale is the thing they're going for. Perish the thought! That's just to get the prospect to the point of being a customer, and to get their name on your house list. **The back-end is the next sale and the next, and that's where you make your money.**

That said, your front-end and back-end systems are actually interlocking components of a complex whole. Once again: **with the front-end system you're bringing people into your marketing funnel. On the back-end, you're nurturing the relationship with those people, and helping those people who give you more and more money.** It's a lot like running an automobile. The front-end is the key that starts the engine; it's small, and doesn't cost much by itself. The back-end system is the fuel that drives the vehicle. It costs a little more, but it's what really drives your business.

In the largest perspective, all this is just marketing — part of the package of things you use to attract and re-attract the best customers. **An effective marketing system is one that does it all for you automatically: the front-end automatically attracts the right people, and a back-end system automatically re-sells them.** I see the front-end/back-end interaction as something like the plate-spinning people you used to see on the Ed Sullivan Show, and that you can still see in some carnivals and circuses. They start spinning those plates, and eventually they get 14 or 15 plates spinning simultaneously. Once they're spinning, all the performer has to do is casually walk back and flip the first one, and then the second, and the third, and so forth. They can keep 15 plates spinning with a minimum of effort — but it does

> Success is the ability to outrun failure!

take effort, or they all come crashing down. That's how it can be for your marketing, too. **You can put systems in place that attract and then re-attract all the best customers, with a minimum of effort on your part.** Think of it as a kind of self-perpetuating money machine.

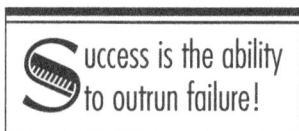

In its simplest manifestation, **your front-end is your lead generation system.** It's the process of taking all the prospects out there and determining which of them you can convert to actual clients. **The back-end becomes the continual marketing to those clients already on your customer list.** The marketing is different for those two aspects of business, since the marketing you'll use to get people to try your service is going to be different from the marketing you'll use to keep selling to the same customers repeatedly. **Ultimately, front-end and back-end marketing systems are the best way to build business and create cash on demand.**

Gaming the System

Like so many of the components of a ruthless marketing system, **front-end/back-end marketing is a systemized way to make on-going, automatic sales.** You should always develop your products and services with this approach in mind, because it's so valuable and proven. My good friend Alan R. Bechtold is in the process of developing a new marketing course, for example, and that's exactly how he's going about it. His new course is based on a series of recorded tele-seminars and a live workshop that he recently conducted. He led a whole group of people through this process in real time, and they each paid a princely sum to be a part of the group; but it goes without saying that it was all recorded, so it could be turned into a course for later use.

First, he recorded five preliminary calls. These calls served two purposes. The first was that they helped those people who paid for the original coaching, and kept them happy until the project officially got started. Second, Alan knew, in the back of his mind, that he was creating a front-end product that he could sell for $17 or $27 — maybe more, maybe less, based on the test marketing — to find prospects who most want to buy the complete course, which he'll sell for a lot more. Now, Alan knows that he'd have very little luck going out to strangers on the street and trying to sell them a course for $997 or $1,499. **But if he sells them the $27 introductory course and follows up with the right pieces, and maybe even a few phone calls, then the sale is very easy** — because he's giving them a chance to get started very inexpensively. Those first five calls and the tons of information on that one CD-ROM make up almost one-third of the course.

Here's a similar example: Video Professor. They have all

these information products that teach you how to use your computer, and what do they do? They offer you the basics on a free disk; all you pay is $6.95 for postage and handling. It's a fantastic method that's used everywhere in the business. **Similarly, almost every infomercial you see is a front-end offer of one type or another. Start paying close attention to those offers.** Call up some of them, and express your interest in buying. Listen to what they have on the back-end, because every offer you see for a low-cost product is a front-end offer, a set-up for the higher-priced back-end offer the marketer derives his profit from.

The idea is to **introduce yourself to the prospect by over-delivering on a low-cost hand-raiser that's worth many times more than what the prospect paid.** At the risk of sounding sexist, **it's a bit like courting a woman.** You may get her attention initially, but you're not going to propose on the first date. Of course, by nurturing that relationship and getting her interested, at some point you can pop the question and expect a reasonable chance of making your "sale." That's what Alan is doing by leading with his $27 offer, and then introducing the bigger course later. His customers are going to be amazed and excited about paying him $1,000 when they think, *Imagine what I can get for $1,000 if I got all this for just $27!* **And here's a point to keep in mind: when making a front-end offer of this sort, be sure to charge something to qualify the prospects.** Otherwise you'll get a lot of people who aren't serious, and some who are will avoid your offer, because they'll think you can't be serious if you're giving it away for free.

Here's something that a lot of people overlook; I've already mentioned it here, but it's worth re-emphasizing. **You have to understand that a front-end sale is simply a customer's entry**

point onto your house list; it's the subsequent sales that are the source of your real profit. I can't tell you how many items I've purchased through the mail, over the Internet, or whatever — and never heard from that vendor again. Obviously, they had

> **You serve yourself best — when you serve others the most.**

no idea what they were doing: they were going for that first sale, and that was it. They got my money, they sent me the product, and it was over; they were on to the next sale. They're spending more money chasing new prospects to get that one front-end sale. It's like the two guys with the potato cart, where at the end of the day they lose money, and they figure, "Well, tomorrow we'll just have to sell more potatoes." But you can get by on fewer new potato sales is you'll just implement a back-end system so you can rake in the profits by selling to previous satisfied customers. Do that, and you're going to have a huge, unfair advantage over 80-90% of the advertisers out there.

Catching a Clue

It's a sad fact of life that most businesses — especially mom-and-pop operations — have no front-end offer to get people in the door. Their philosophy seems to be, "OK, I'm located at 608 Main Street here and I have a sign in the window that says OPEN FOR BUSINESS. That should be enough." Well, that's the wrong approach. **You need a front-end offer to get people into your store — or if you're a service provider, a reason to get them to call your business.** It should be something that costs you very little, but has a high perceived value. Don't make the mistake of either having no front-end, or of having a shoddy front-end that nobody wants. On the other hand, it shouldn't cost you too much to sell it at a big discount or give it away for free.

If you're a business owner, you have to keep asking yourself, over and over again, **"What's next?"** I think you should even put it on you wall in 200-point type, where you can look at it all the time: "What's next?" When you've got somebody who's interested and passionate about whatever it is you're selling — whether it's knitting supplies or Army boots — those people are insatiable. They'll keep buying and rebuying. It's up to you, though: **the responsibility is on your shoulders to keep dreaming up new things to sell them.**

Most business owners are either out there chasing the next sale, and wearing themselves out in the process, or they're not doing anything. **Remember Russ von Hoelscher's story** about the printer who worked in the strip center close to his office? He was always complaining about how there was never enough business. Russ finally told him, "Look, you've got to get some people in — there are hundreds of businesses within a mile of here. Paper them with flyers, go after the business, and be aggressive." But the printer said something amazingly stupid: "Look, pal. I'm open for business. I've got a printing press. If they want printing, they can come to me."

Now, he's on the backside of a strip mall, and he's unwilling to make that effort to sell his product. That's an absolute recipe for disaster, and it's hard to feel sorry for him! But **he verbalized the way that most people think, as rotten as that attitude is.** That kind of attitude will only work if you've got a printing press back there and you intend to *print* the money you need to survive. Or, hey, you could print your own "GOING OUT OF BUSINESS" sign. Why not?

In my experience, the people who have that attitude are, for the most part, the people who've opened a business because that's what they've always dreamed of doing. They're already going into it with an attitude that they're the king on the throne, ruling over their new kingdom — their business — and the great unwashed masses are just going to come through the door and be thankful that they've thrown the "OPEN" sign in the window. Sorry, that's not the way it works. It's true that there are some people who do that and actually make a profit, but that only works under certain circumstances; if you have a dynamite location and you give good service, you might be able to survive, a least temporarily. But even if you do, you're losing so much more. If you're not serving the customers properly, you're leaving room for someone to come in take them all away.

If, on the other hand, you'll do the things I'm talking about here, you won't just survive — you'll thrive. It's easy: offer a great, cheap offer to get them to come in the first time, let them get comfortable with you and understand a little about your business, then hit them with your back-end offer. Try handing out samples, if your business is amenable to that kind of thing. If you've got a hairdressing salon, offer a $5 perm. Once they're in, make sure you over-deliver, and they're going to be back.

Servicing the Client

Even if you have a great front-end offer that you over-deliver on, you can't count on every customer to come back on his own. **A good front-end system is useless unless you couple it with an effective back-end system, so you can take advantage of that goodwill and sense of reciprocity you've generated with your front-end offer.** What comes next is a regular, systematic communication that goes out to those customers and gives them a specific reason to keep coming back and buying from you. **Even the people who know how valuable a customer list is are losing a whole lot of money that should be theirs, simply because they're not aggressively re-inviting their customers to come back and buy from them on a regular basis.**

You see, your customers are (silently) begging to be acknowledged. They want to be nurtured; they want to be responded to. If you take that first order and do nothing with it, then you're doing a great disservice to the customer. So the obligation you have as a marketer is to massage the egos of your customers, and help them give you more reasons to serve them. **So many times we worry about making that first sale, when in reality it's our ability to help our customers improve their lives, fulfill their desires, and solve their problems that's important.** We do that by continually offering them new products, related products, and related services. They may not even know what direction to go in after they've bought that initial product; so if you just pitch them something at that point, they'll probably come back and buy from you again. So what if it costs you a cent for a postcard and a few cents for postage? **That's just a dollar or so per customer per year, and those who respond will spend at least a hundred times that on repeat business with you.** What business owner wouldn't exchange a dollar for a hundred dollars every day, and as many times during that day as they possibly could?

> **You can't have the glory... IF YOU DON'T HAVE THE GUTS!**

Now, this goes right back to what I said earlier about what you, as a marketer, should always be asking yourself: **"What's next?"** The customer is *already* asking that question, even before you ask it yourself. Sometimes they're asking it even as they purchase that first product. In other words, **they're looking for reasons to do more business with you,** and you've got to be able to answer that question instantly.

An Offer They Can't Refuse

The combination of aggressive front-end and back-end marketing works well with just about any advertising medium, from the Internet and direct mail to infomercials. Just combine this method with the other techniques in this book, especially Direct Response Marketing, and you've got yourself a well-oiled moneymaking machine.

In order for this strategy to work most effectively, however, **you've got to start out with an excellent, high-value offer that your prospect will think they'd have to be a fool to refuse.** A lot of us in the business accomplish this by offering a free report or even a free book as a lead generator. If you want to charge a dollar or two for the book, go ahead; most people appreciate things they have to pay for. But in the case of a report, which is really a glorified sales letter, just give it away free. That'll bring a whole bunch of people into your funnel (you remember the funnel, don't you?).

Let's say I'm selling a book distributorship; I'd offer them the distributorship for several hundreds of dollars on the back-end. **But like most people who market information products, I use a 1-2-3 approach with most items.** That is, **1)** to get the people into the funnel, **2)** to make a medium-sized sale on the back-end, and then — the third spoke on the wheel is the most important — **3)** offer them an even bigger package: maybe reprint or resell rights for a bunch of tapes and books, at a price that could be $1,000 or more.

My friend Russ von Hoelscher has owned a number of retail bookstores. An effective offer he once used was to have people sign up for a $250 free book-shopping spree every month. All three of the stores he operated at the time used the promotion in their ads, and that enticed people in. There was no obligation, and no purchase necessary. They just signed a card and dropped it into a big bowl. But Russ found that with book customers, even browsers — well, they couldn't just come in and drop the card. They'd start looking at the books, and Russ would often get a sale. Another thing he did, when faced with heavy competition from some of the huge conglomerate bookstores, was to give away, at cost, his top ten bestsellers. It was an effective strategy; he never made much profit with them anyhow. **But by giving a discount of 40% off — literally giving them away at cost — people would come in to get the hot books, but then they'd go deeper in the store**. They'd look at some of the other books and audio programs, and often they'd leave not just with a couple of bestsellers, but two or three other items that made Russ a nice profit.

That brings to mind an especially effective front-end/back-end offer that a lot of different businesses can and do use: **a low-cost yearly membership that includes a free report or a free product.** You see this kind of thing at Barnes & Noble and at large record stores all the time, but it could be used with just about any business. You start out with a good front-end that leads to bigger and bigger back-end purchases, plus customer loyalty. **When people are members of something, they feel better about themselves and what they're buying.** Remember, people want to feel important. It's almost like they're running around with these invisible signs flashing, "MAKE ME FEEL

IMPORTANT, PLEASE!"

We all want to feel special. **When you make your customers members of something, or give them some association they can join, the real purpose is to develop them as customers and to sell them more stuff.** If they're a part of some membership, it makes them feel like they have that inside angle or that inside scoop on everyone else. And to a certain extent, they should. **You should segment your client list so that your "Gold" or "Platinum" customers get an especially nice deal** — for example, a sharp discount, or maybe you open the store only for them on particular days. That can really get some excitement going.

Now, maybe at its root the whole membership thing is phony, since you're more interested in them spending their money than in developing a club — but the more real you make it, the better. Then you're able to educate the customers. If you're selling knitting supplies or beads or books, you can

> **P**eople hate to be "sold" — but they love to "choose."

have all kinds of workshops and seminars and bring in book authors to speak. **You can do all kinds of things to get people more addicted to whatever it is that you're selling.**

If you don't have a club for them to join, then have people come in and sign up for a drawing to win a grand prize, the way Russ did. Of course, only one person will win that; but by the end of the promotion, you'll have captured the names of everybody who participated. Remarkably, everyone can be a second-place winner, and get a discount on whatever you're selling! Just send them a little letter that says, "Unfortunately, you're not a first-place winner, but..." and then play up the fact that they *did* win second place. Little do they know that everybody else did too — but that's not important. **Coming in second it makes them feel important; it makes them feel appreciated; and again, it gives them a reason to come back in.**

Here's another thing that a contest does, as it relates to the front-end. **The only people who sign up for any kind of contest are those who are already interested in whatever the prize is that you're giving away.** In my first business, I tried everything to get customers. You name it, I tried it — as long as it didn't cost very much; after all, I was on a limited budget. I used to knock on doors till my knuckles bled. **The one method that worked best for me was a giveaway.** This was when I had a carpet cleaning business, by the way — several years before I got into mail order and information products. I had a contest that ran continually, to give away three rooms of carpet cleaning, absolutely free. I put these little boxes up in different places around town, and I'd go collect my leads every day. I'd call them up and I'd give them the bad news, which was that they didn't get the three free rooms worth of cleaning. The *good* news was that they'd won the consolation prize, which was conditional. I'd do some free work for them if they would take a minimum amount of other work. Then, once I got in their house, I'd try to run the bill up as high as I could. I was closing between 30% and 50% of all of the people who were signing up for the contest, and the reason **I was closing those people is because they were pre-qualified to begin with.** Only a fool would enter a contest to get three rooms of free carpet cleaning, if they weren't interested in getting that done.

You can always make your consolation prize a lead generation tool, where they get so much off the goods and services you're selling. If you're working with a women's clothing store, like my friend Kris Solie-Johnson, you can run a contest where the winner gets a free outfit, while all the second-place prizewinners get 20% off all their purchases. But you can sweeten the pot a little, too; so why not offer 25%-30 off their purchases if the second-place prizewinner brings in friend who hasn't been to the store before? **Set it up that way, and you'll have customers bringing in customers who are like them,** people you *know* will like what you have to offer — because why would you bring one of your girlfriends to a store if you knew she'd hate the clothes? This can work not only to bring in more customers, but to get everybody back into the store a second time.

You Can't Have a Front Without a Back

Here's something I wished I'd known when I got started: make sure, **once you've got that front-end attractor in place, that you've got something to back it up with.** Once that's system's in place to attract new customers, you've got to have your "What's next?" ready to offer to that new customer as the back-end sale. Let me say this again: **you need to have that decided and worked out before you even think about making that first offer to the customer, or your front-end can backfire on you!**

The last thing you want to do is to get all excited and worked up about your front-end and then go scrambling to find a back-end to offer your customers. Oh, you can certainly do it that way, but it's a pain. Instead of scrambling when you get that first order, instead of running around trying to figure out what you're going to do, you need to have that already mapped out in your marketing model. **You want to put that offer in the fulfillment package for the front-end product.** In other words, whatever it is you're using for your front-end sale — whether it's a book or a report or free yarn — when they open that package up, there needs to be that back-end offer staring them right in the face. **Because, remember, people are going to be asking themselves right away, "What's next?" And you want to be there with the answer.**

That's one of the reasons that I love information products: because you can always use a piece of that information product as your front-end, and you know already what your back-end is. But if yours is a physical product, consider the possibility of planning your front-end offer from the back-end offer. You need your goal — *What am I going to do?* — on the front-end to get them in. What will raise that hand? **Now, the worst thing you can do is let that hand-raiser get cold.** They're eager to buy *now*. They've just met you, and they're excited about you. They're more excited about you when you deliver that front-end product than they will be for the rest of your relationship, probably. Why on Earth would you wait and let them cool off for three weeks while you think of what else you're going to offer them? **You want another offer to go in there — preferably with the front-end package, but if nothing else, immediately following.**

Here's another tip: **never have a front-end offer that isn't related to the back-end.** I don't just think that's important, I think it's *essential.* Your front-end offer must dovetail with your back-end approach; otherwise, the person raising their hand isn't necessarily interested in what you're going to sell on the back-end. In fact, in many cases, your back-end can be the same product as your front-end; for example

> **C**ustomers go where they are invited and stay where they are appreciated.

vitamins or supplements. **The front-end sale is the product, and the back-end sale is more of the same.** Sometimes you can get the back-end sale at the same time you make the front-end sale, but that's a whole other strategy.

Think it all through so that **your front-end gives them a small sampling of what they're going to get, so they get to like it.** Be like the Chick-Fil-A or Mrs. Fields cookie people; they're out there passing out free samples. The people who take those samples say, "Thank you" and walk about 20 steps, and all of a sudden they turn around and come back and buy a dozen cookies.

What the Heck *is* a System, Anyway?

Now, *there's* a question that's been begging to be asked: what is a system? **By definition, it's a group of interacting or interrelated parts that make up a whole.** When you're developing a front- or back-end system, at first glance the whole thing may seem overwhelming; it may seem too complex for you. **The best thing to do is to look at this system as a set of pieces that all fit together to create, first, that front-end system, and then the associated back-end system.**

Your front-end system is designed to promote new products, or generate leads, or sell an order to a first-time customer. But within that front-end system, you may have a series of mini-systems that compose the system itself. Maybe you've got a mini-system that generates leads for your business; then you might have a system in place that you use to create a new offer or new products for customers. Then, of course, you may as well have a system that sells the prospect. Maybe it's your Direct Mail System, where you regularly and systematically contact those leads on a week-to-week or month-to-month or semi-annual basis.

The back-end, of course, is the system where the real money really is. It's designed to ethically extract money from the pockets of clients and customers and prospects, and put that money into your bank account — into your own pocket. (Notice, again, that it's important that you do this ethically — if not because you want a clear conscience, then at least because you don't want your misdeeds to jump up and bite you on the ass someday.) You might have a mini-system within your back-end system that progressively and aggressively follows up with your clients every 15 or 30 days. **If you do that systematically, you're going to see your sales and your profits grow substantially.**

The secret is to bridge the gap between that front-end system and the associated back-end system. **The front-end system lets you leverage off your knowledge of your industry, your experience, your background, what you do best; the back-end system lets you leverage off what you know about your clients.** It's important that you have a system in place that lets the clients tell you what they want. As the old saying goes, "The only votes that count are the ones that are paid for," and your customers vote by paying for products that you offer on the front-end. You know that on the back-end, you're going to offer them more and more products related to that first purchase.

Most business people are too focused on the front-end, though, to ever make any money on the back-end. They get so excited about making that first sale that it's just like almost being on a narcotics high. But what happens when the sale is over? They've got to immediately go get another high by making another sale. In doing that, they're just leaving money on the table. If they would just work the back-end properly, they could create five or ten times more income and business for their company. You see, **your largest marketing expense is always new-customer acquisition. The easiest business is selling to people who already trust you, who've already bought from you.** Knowing that, you want to create products on the back-end that appeal to those people.

A good example of a back-end system is what happens at Amazon.com. If you go there and buy a book, that's the front-end. But when go through the process of purchasing that book, you're going to see a page that says, "People who bought this book also bought..." Well, that's a back-end offer. Or you may go to a concert, and spend $70 for a ticket. When you get there, they're going to try to sell you a T-shirt, a cap, a CD, or something else. That's the back end. You may end up spending $150 or even more, all told.

> Go out of your way to show people that you are REAL and vulnerable — and they will emotionally open up to you.

The question is, how do you develop a good back-end system? First if all, take a good look at your business. What do you sell to your customers? What are they interested in? Can you upsell them — that is, can you get them to buy something bigger and better? Can you cross-sell to them — can you get them to buy something that's related to that product that you sold them on the front-end? **The ideas you come up with will help you create a back-end system for your business.**

I look at as being it like riding a bike up a tall hill. That's the vision I have of getting new customers. Man, it's difficult! I'm riding that bike up on a hot summer day, and I'm pedaling and I'm breathing hard, and I can't even ride all the way. I actually have to get off and walk the bike up the rest of the way. But then, when it comes to reselling those customers again and again, it's like coasting that bike right down the same hill. I've got my arms up like you do on a roller coaster ride, and I'm not even putting in any effort: I'm zipping right on down the hill. **The fun part of the business is *not* getting the first sale. The fun part of the business is developing relationships with customers who love you and trust you, who let you get inside their heads and inside their hearts.** You get to know them better than they know themselves; and then, whatever you want to sell them, **you create the money at will.**

You've got to realize in business that you're going to spend a certain amount of money to acquire any customer. All your customers come with a price, whether it's what you spend in ads, or what you spend in time and energy to attract them. But it's worth it if you can figure out the average lifetime revenue of every new customer you acquire. You can literally lose money in the short-term while attracting your customers, if you determine that their value, down the road, is many times more than what you're spending now.

Let me reiterate: *you can afford to lose money on your front-end sale.* You can sell something at less than your cost, if you must. A good 90% of your competition won't do this, because they won't do anything that affects their bottom line. But if you lose a few bucks on the front-end to entice people to come to you, and *then* have great, related items that you can make a huge profit on — then so what if you lose money on the front-end? **There's tons of money to be had on the back-end.** The most important part of this is knowing what the lifetime value of the average customer is. If you know that, you can go negative on the front-end, because you know that you're going to recover any losses.

Some people call these kinds of offers "loss-leaders." I prefer to think of them as investments towards future profits. If you do everything possible to know your best customers intimately, and make them the kinds of repeat offers that you know they'll be attracted to, you'll make money hand over fist.

But Why Doesn't Everyone Use This Method?

Some people are just too softhearted for their own good to make a system like this work. This all sounds somewhat ruthless — because you're trying to extract every last dollar of disposable income from your customers. But if you're providing products and services that represent true value to your marketplace, then there's nothing ruthless about it. It's more *aggressive* than anything. **I wish more business people would realize the tremendous amount of money they're losing by failing to vigorously resell to their customers.** As a business owner, you should always try to do more business with people who've already shown a certain level of trust in you.

Then again, many business people feel that the high point in their business is getting that first customer. They've never developed the art and science of attracting customers, and they never will. But if you know your system and your customers well enough that you can lose money on the front-end — if you know the lifetime value of your customers, and really nurture relationships with them and help them become not just customers but an integral part of your own life — then there's value there for everyone. **The problem with most marketers today is that they only see the quick money, the upfront money, the easy money.** They want the get-rich-quick money — when in reality, getting rich is in the *back-end*. It's in the long-term. And hey, let's be honest about it: **a lot of marketers are just flat-out lazy.**

They don't want to go through all the necessary steps, and they don't want to take the initiative to do those things that need to be done to make it a business instead of just a hobby.

> **T**he best product does not always win, *but the best marketing always does!*

Another part of the problem may simply be that things have changed in the business world in the last few decades, and people haven't gotten used thinking about, much less using, this new way of doing business. Twenty years ago, if you were the only grocery store on the corner, people went there. Think of it as the Field of Dreams business model: "If you build it, they will come." **But there are so many choices today that we've gotten a bit jaded and cynical about the different marketing messages we see. So the smaller business owner, especially the home-based business, needs to stand out from everybody else out there.** The Field of Dreams business model is mostly dead in America. You have to compete vigorously, and provide additional services that the Big Box companies aren't going to provide.

The key is establishing reciprocal relationships with your customers so your business can survive in the long-term. Let's say you're a novice knitter, and you don't know how to cast off the needles. You're not going to go to Wal-Mart and have someone show you how to do that — because, frankly, they're not going to. You have to go to a smaller neighborhood store that's going to have some of the personal service that the Big Boxes lack, a place that's willing to build a relationship with you. But if they don't pitch to you and don't market to you, you may not know what to ask them. **Whereas, if a little knitting store regularly sends you a postcard to tell you they have beginner**

classes or new types of yarns, they're educating you, and you'll probably spend more money with them. Therefore you'll enjoy your hobby more, and they'll get more sales — it's win-win all around.

Hubba Hubba!

Sometimes **it's the worst things in life that provide the best examples,** if only so we can draw parallels to the good things. **So I'm going to discuss pornography** for a while. I realize it's a controversial subject, and I'm going to keep this PG-rated all the way. But there's this story I heard a long time ago; I've never forgotten it, and I think it illustrates something very important when it comes to understanding the power of front-end and back-end marketing. It's the story of Hugh Hefner.

As most people know, Hugh Hefner was the man who started *Playboy* magazine in the early 1950's. At that time, it was a revolutionary idea — though maybe "revolutionary" is the wrong word, because some people are so anti-porn that they may think it was a *terrible* idea. But in any case, it was new; let's just put it that way. Hefner was the first to go this route, and he was very insecure about the fate of his little publication — which, by the way, is rather innocent by today's standards. My wife gets the Victoria's Secrets catalog in the mail, and it's a lot racier... not that I ever look at it or anything!

Anyhow, the first *Playboy* was very innocent compared to today, but at that time it was new and unprecedented. Hefner was so unsure about it that he didn't even print a date on his first publication, since he figured it might just sit on the newsstands for a year or two before it sold out. He printed 5,000 copies, hoping that he wasn't going to lose all his money. But all 5,000 copies sold out in just a few days, and the rest is history.

Some people saw his success and started saying, "Hey, here's a guy who's found a new market!" One of the very first magazines to take him on was *Penthouse*. The story I heard was that when *Penthouse* went into business to compete against *Playboy*, all the experts in the publishing world said, "Look, there's no way this marketplace is big enough for two of these magazines. There's just absolutely no way!" And they did everything possible to advise the people behind *Penthouse* not to do it. "Don't spend your money! The marketplace just isn't big enough for two!" Now, of course, we can see what a ridiculous statement *that* was. Nowadays there isn't just *Playboy* and *Penthouse*; there are about a hundred other publications out there, and some are really quite pornographic.

Here's my point. It has nothing, really, to do with pornography, except as a means of illustration. The point is that **people are insatiable. They can't get enough!** The person who collects one gun is going to have a dozen before long. If there was just one fishing book on the market, that would be ridiculous, because readers would have an insatiable appetite for more — and so there's hundreds of them. The same's true for poker books, and hunting, and stamp collecting. **We're a nation of people who get involved with something and want more, more, more.**

Certain products and services lend themselves more to this emotional intensity than others. Look at casinos. When the government made it so that any Indian tribe in the country could start a casino, everybody said, "Well, there's the end of Vegas. There's the end of Atlantic City." When VCRs first came out in the 1980s, all kinds of people were saying, "There goes the movie industry." When it became possible to download free music on the Internet, all the experts said, "There goes the whole music industry right there. People can get it for free." Well, as you know, none of that has happened. **The marketplace is absolutely, positively *insatiable*, and the people buying this stuff from you right now will buy from you again and again, *if* you make them the right offers and make it easy for them.**

> **N**egative motivation often works <u>much</u> <u>better</u> than anything positive! The stick is always better than the carrot!

The problem is that **you have to be creative enough to come up with all kinds of different products and services that somehow relate to what you're selling** — and it really does take some creativity. You can do exactly what Hugh Hefner and all those other guys have done, only you don't have to do it with something like pornography. **You can build an empire! You can resell, and you can copy someone who's doing something right.** This is especially useful for the small business owner. Find out what your competitor is doing. If he's making a lot of money doing something, you want to do the same thing — only try to do it better than he does. **Don't steal from them, but borrow their best principles.** Even what some people would consider old, crowded markets can be revitalized if you work them right.

The bottom line is that the market is absolutely insatiable. If you grow a garden, next year you'll want to know how to grow a better garden. If you raise a rabbit, you'll like to know how to breed rabbits and sell them to other people. In other words, you — the customer — want to know more. One key to success is *not* looking for the place where there's no competition, **but focusing on the place where there *is* competition that's**

making money in spite of the fact that they don't understand front-end/back-end marketing — places where they aren't even using those techniques but are still raking in the cash. Now you can step in and dominate that category and they'll be left in the dust, shaking their heads, going, "Wow! What happened here?"

So if you're looking to start a new business, **look for the places where there are plenty of competitors, because that shows just how rabid the market is.** You want to find a market that's not only hungry, but spending money too. **Look for people already making money in spite of the fact that they don't know what you know.** Let's go back to the pornography example for a minute. My wife once asked me, "What's wrong with men? Don't they realize that when you've seen one picture of a naked woman, you've seen it all?" And she's right — what else is there to see? But this illustrates the fact that people buy for emotional reasons. If everybody thought logically, then you'd see a picture of a naked person and you'd say, "Oh, well, that's interesting," and that would be it. But people can never get enough. While there are certain markets that are more prone to this insatiability, everybody buys for emotional, not logical, reasons. **It's up to you as the business owner to determine what those emotional reasons are, so you can use that as your ammunition and go out and try to get every disposable dollar you can from your customer base.**

There are a few businesses that, at first glance, you might think are *not* emotional — and I've run one. That would be carpet cleaning. But believe it or not, carpet cleaning can be a very emotional thing, because most of my customers were women. Generally, men couldn't care less about whether or not their carpets are dirty; my female customers, on the other hand, were all extremely emotionally attached to their homes. Their homes were important to them, and the more involved they were with social life, they more deeply they cared about what all their friends, family, and neighbors thought. Anybody walking through their home was judging them by the appearance of their home, after all. Once I really got into the heads and hearts of these people, it was so easy to go in there for a $50 job and walk out with a couple of hundred dollars; all I would have to do was point out a few little things here and there. It's all about learning where you can squeeze those emotional triggers.

People buy stuff that excites them more than they buy stuff that they just need. But it's important to point out that they select among the competitors even for those items that they need, and those selections are *still* made for emotional reasons. That's why your message — your offer of a free or inexpensive trial — is important. Now they're getting something for nothing.

Setting Up the Systems

Let's talk a little bit about setting up your own front-end and back-end systems. What I'd like you to do is take out a piece of paper and make three different columns on it. Make one column for low-cost items — typically something that's free or up to about $20-25. The middle column is for items in the $100 range. Make the last column for big-ticket stuff — $500-1000. For every business, you should be able to come up with different ideas about what you can offer in each of these categories, and as I go on, I'll give you examples of brick-and-mortar businesses and how this relates to them.

Next, start brainstorming ideas for different types of products that you put in each one of those columns — **because if you set up the system with the back-end *before* you set up the**

front-end, you'll end up with a continuous flow of products.
Once you've got new customers in, you don't have to scramble
around trying to figure out something for the back-end. In the
beginning, focus on free or low-cost items. The Video Professor
example I mentioned earlier is a great one; it's a free CD with
information on it — though it does cost $6.95 for shipping and
handling. But even though they have to pay shipping and
handling, the customer still sees that as a free product. **So your
front-end offering, at least in the beginning, should be a free
or low-cost item that's very easy for you to deliver.** You don't
want to get into something that's complicated to deliver, because
that will just eat away at your profit margin.

The second thing you want to **focus on is something that's
of very high value to your prospect or customer.** Look at
information — maybe insider information. I discussed the
usefulness of memberships earlier:

> ise men have
> many doubts.

about how valuable it is to make people
feel important that they're insiders, that
they're really part of something, maybe
even a part of history. **Give them information that can change
their business.**

I want to make it clear that this isn't the place to give away
junk — say, something that wasn't selling very well, or that you
couldn't even give away. If new customers start receiving junk,
they'll assume that the rest what you have to offer is junk, and
that they shouldn't pay any more for whatever else you have.
**Your front-end could be some part of a high-end product that
you're going to give away,** like the first chapter of a book, or the
first few tele-seminars in the beginning of a course. Offers like
these really lead people to buy the higher-end product.

After you brainstorm all of these categories, you can start crafting different offers. **How can these items work together?** What would the flow of one to the other to the next be like? The last step, of course, is finding other businesses that offer your type of product, and studying them for pointers.

Let me give you just a couple of examples of good front-end/back-end systems I've heard of recently. A local library offered a summer reading program for kids, and if the kids read so many books they got a free cookie at a place called the Great Harvest Bread Company. Since the librarian tells kids that they get this free cookie if they read books, they not only read the books, but they become a pain in the butt to their parents to go get that free cookie. When the parents take their kids to go to get this free cookie, they can't just walk into the Great Harvest Bread Company and ask for a free cookie. They have to buy a loaf of bread, too. The bread is $3.50, so suddenly that "free" cookie has cost them cost them $3.50. And if the Great Harvest Bread Company took their names and addresses at that point, they could continue to offer the parents different products by mailings — and the parents might listen. After all, they know where the store is; they've been there before. The people there were nice to their kids — they gave them free cookies — so the parents will probably continue to go back.

Here's how the front-end/back-end worked in this example. First they got the customer in with free cookies, then they upsold to the $3.50 bread. Now it's time to move up to the mid-category, the $100 range. That may be something like a year's supply of bread that the customer pays for at the beginning of a 12-month period. Maybe it's a membership — a "Bread of the Month" Club. There may also be other things they can try to get that customer to give them more and more money, as a result of their initial "free cookies for kids" program.

As you can see, **there are many different things out there that businesses can do to generate business.** If you start mapping out, in the beginning, some of the low-cost, mid-cost, and high-end things that you as a business owner can offer people, you can quickly create a good, step-by-step path from beginning to end, so you're not trying to come up with something all of a sudden later.

Here's a handy tip: **be sure to get it all down on paper.** So many times we try to internalize these things and juggle them in our minds, when really the best thing is to document it all. **Create a flow chart of how the different elements of the system are interconnected.** What makes one work? What makes it work better? Then you can see the flow of money. If you're constantly creating value, you're constantly going to be getting maximum income from each of your customers.

Here's another thing. Unless we put something on paper, it may be that everything I'm saying here just sounds like a great idea. You're going to read this chapter, it's all going to be somewhat entertaining to you, and then you're just going to forget about it. **For this to work, you have to document your strategies and implement them.** My best advice for implementation is to do what I've been trying to do for a number of years: get up every morning and try to focus on your business before all the workaday interruptions get started, before all the distractions get in the way. **Try to think these things through, to develop a plan. Use these very clear, step-by-step strategies to do it, and for goodness sake, write it all down!** That's the best piece of advice I can give you.

A Backup Back-End

One of the most useful things about mapping things out in detail and documenting them is the fact that you can include a plan for those people who won't take you up on that first offer — a backup back-end offer, if you will. Maybe it's a lower price; maybe it's got more bonuses or more value than your other offer; maybe it's something related, but in a sub-category in a different direction. In a week or two, after you've seen whether your customers have responded or not, **you can take those same people who raised their hands in the first place and give them another shot at doing business with you. You know they're going to want to do business with you, because they're pleased with what you over-delivered for the $10 or $20 they gave you to start out with.** You don't want to let them sit too long and forget who you are. I think it's a good idea to make sure your plan branches out. **Make contingencies.** If they *do* buy your backup back-end offer, do you then send them a higher-end offer, and when? If they don't buy that, do you send them another offer that's going to move them into the funnel better? **More to the point, if you have multiple items in your low-cost and mid-cost categories and one isn't working, you can try another.**

In any case, **it's important to keep going after them.** You might think it's a pain to keep getting

---

General George Patton had one simple rule for warfare that works like magic in business. **Every battle plan must be carried out with 3 things:**
- ➤ **Speed!**
- ➤ **Simplicity!**
- ➤ **Boldness!**

Your marketing plans must incorporate these 3 elements. Strike FAST, strike HARD, and strike OFTEN!

---

postcards from the same realtor, over and over, month after month — but when you're ready to sell the house you're living in, who are you going to call? Probably the agent who sent you 25 or 30 postcards over the years. So don't give up. Keep sending; stay in touch with your customers, because the more you stay in touch with them, the more likely they are going to respond to you if you have something they want. And make them specific offers every time. You're not just staying in touch with them, asking them to call you for no reason; **you're telling them** *exactly* **what you want them to do. You're telling them** *exactly* **what's in it for them. When they do respond to you, they're doing it for a very clear and compelling reason.**

The best part about all this is that once you've got them with your front-end offer, it doesn't matter if you're not the best copywriter in the world. At that point **your copy doesn't have to be perfect,** because you already know they're interested in what you have. Chances are, they're going to want more of it — they're going to be asking, "What's next?" So don't worry about being a world-class copywriter; just whip out a sales letter talking about your next product and send it to them, because you've already broken the ice with that front-end offer. I've said it before and I'll probably say it again: **good enough is good enough.**

The Sum of Its Parts

There's an old marketing question every business owner should ask himself: "Am I in the business of making sales?" And the answer is: No, **you're in the business of building relationships with customers.** When you develop that relationship, you'll have a pool of customers ready and eager to buy whatever it is you have to sell. **Isn't that worth developing a front-end system?**

The answer is yes. Earlier, I mentioned the fact that a lot of business people are lazy. Well, if you're lazy — and we all have that streak in us — then you should be excited about what I've gone over in this chapter, because **doing well in this business is really about developing relationships.** The front-end — the things you do to attract the best prospects, those who are most likely to end up doing business with you in the future — is just the beginning. It's a necessary evil, and it's a lot of hard work. But then comes the real business of making money: the back-end business, where you're building relationships. **For those of us who are lazy, this is the easiest money you'll ever make because all you're doing is being a friend.** People will do things for their friends that they won't do for anybody else; when somebody has a relationship with you, there's a trust built up there. **They'll do whatever you ask them to do, as long as they trust you enough and as long as they believe in you enough.** Really, that's all this is about. It's the easiest money you'll ever make in your life.

6

Develop a Deep Understanding of Your Target Market

This is our greatest secret, the one I believe served us best when we first got started. **You see, although we were new to the business itself, we were already very familiar with the market.** I was 28 years old; my wife Eileen was 30. This was back in 1988, when we were just a couple of kids who had never made more than $26,000 a year combined. **I had a little carpet-cleaning business at the time, and that's how I met Eileen:** I stopped in at the filling station where she was working for minimum wage and asked for directions. I was looking for a street that was just two blocks long, and I thought it was in the area where her filling station was. As it turned out, it was on the other side of town, but I still got lucky: I met the woman who would become my wife of 22 years. We started dating, and she was the only girlfriend I'd ever had who actually wanted to come with me on my carpet-cleaning jobs. Even though she had multiple sclerosis, and still does, she would come along and do all the physically demanding work it took to do those jobs. **I actually fell in love with her on one of those jobs!**

By then, I'd had the carpet-cleaning business for about two years. All that time (and for years before) I'd also been sending away for all kinds of moneymaking plans and programs, and I had all these moneymaking ideas in my head. Luckily, Eileen was very ambitious; she was looking for an opportunity, too. **When I told her about my plans for getting rich, her eyes just lit up. Even though I could barely afford a roof over my head at the time, she knew that it *was* possible to get rich — and so did I.**

We had nothing going for us at all. I wasn't even a high school graduate. I went and got my G.E.D. because my dad insisted that I do so, but I didn't even have a real diploma. Eileen had graduated from high school, but she never went to college. We were dirt poor. And yet Eileen saw me sending away for all of these plans and opportunities, and she got excited about some of them. That was in 1987. **We were trying different moneymaking plans, we were joining multilevel marketing companies, and I saw that she was the kind of woman that I could work side-by-side with.** She wasn't one of those women who was always critical, cutting down all my ideas — and that was part of the key to our success. I think having a spouse who's supportive is vitally important.

Before we met, Eileen didn't know anything about the opportunity market. But when she started seeing all these crazy sales letters I was getting, and the fact that I was spending all my money on these programs, she got it in a big way. **I remember her telling me, "T.J., the way to get rich is to be in this business. We need to come up with a plan of our own to sell."** That was incredibly insightful of her. She saw all these plans and programs, and she saw that most of them were total crap; that was obvious because I lost money on most of them. Her telling me, "I think the way to get rich is to actually *sell* these plans and programs," was what changed our lives for the better.

About nine months after we got married, **we took two programs we really liked, programs that we thought were a cut above the others, and combined them in a unique way to make**

> # Money may not make you happy... but it will help calm your nerves! It's always better to have it and not need it than to need it and not have it!

a little booklet — more of a brochure, really. It was a terrible little thing, filled with typographical errors, that embarrasses me to look at to this day. It was called *Dialing for Dollars*. **Then we took $300 that we'd earned from selling a beat-up old carpet-cleaning van and ran a one-sixth page ad in a moneymaking magazine to advertise our program.** That was September 1988. **Within less than five years, *Dialing for Dollars* had brought in over $10 million.**

We had a lot of help along the way, and it took a lot of hard work, but **one of the most important factors in our success was that we were familiar with the market,** even if we didn't know it. Like I said, I'd been sending away for all these plans, programs, and opportunities for years. I was what we lovingly call an "opportunity junkie" — I couldn't get enough. Little did I know that there were millions of people out there just like me. **This is a very lucrative market — and before we got started in the market, we already knew a lot about it.**

That first little ad was the spark that started our mighty fire — and it took me a whole weekend to write it. I knew that we only had $300, and that we could only run a one-sixth page ad, which today will probably cost you $500 to 600. **I knew we had a limited amount of space, and the ad had to be just right —**

because if we didn't get off to a good start, there went *that* idea. So, it took me a whole weekend to write this little, tiny ad. I laid it out like all the other little ads that I'd seen running forever, and I ran it. **We used the profits from that ad to buy two more, and the profits from those two ads to buy four; then we built to eight and sixteen, and *then* we started running full-page ads. Eventually we started doing direct-mail and card-pack advertising, and we just kept expanding.**

We got a lot of help from a lot of good people along the way. The first person who helped us in a big way was Russ von Hoelscher, a man I now consider one of our mentors. Now, Russ didn't help us out of the goodness of his heart! **He started out as a consultant, and we had to pay him thousands of dollars for his help.** This is a business, and time is the one element that is precious to us all. It's a limited resource we can never get back once it's spent.

The opportunity market is the best-kept secret out there, and we didn't even realize it at the time. **It's such a lucrative market.** There are millions of rabid buyers, people who are just like I was for years, people who are sending away for every single plan and program they can. I call it the second largest niche marketplace in the world. Now, let me explain that to you. **First of all, a market is simply a group of people who have something in common.** This commonality causes them to feel and act a certain way, which causes them to buy certain kinds of products and services — and to rebuy them. **There are people in the opportunity market who are multi-millionaires.** They're just looking for the next million-dollar deal, or they're bored, or they want to get into something new. Some of them are doctors and lawyers who are sick and tired of their professions, or now they're retired and they want to try something else. **And on the**

other end of the scale, there are people who are illiterate. I'm not being judgmental; it's just a fact. They can't read or write and they're on welfare. **I was somewhere in the middle of the field. I was dead broke, sending away for all these moneymaking plans and programs, and yet I had a small business and I was fully committed to being an entrepreneur. I was doing the best I knew how, even though I wasn't making very much money.**

There are reasons why we were able to turn $300 into $10 million in our first four years. **First of all, we were very familiar with the market. We also had a lot of help from a lot of people, and we were willing to do whatever it took to succeed.** I like to call us the "Forrest Gumps." Remember the movie with Tom Hanks? Whatever you told Forrest Gump to do he did, and he ended up becoming a multi-millionaire and having a great life. He just did what he was told: He didn't question it. **That's how it was for Eileen and me.** When Russ von Hoelscher first came along and started working with us, whatever Russ told us to do, we just did it. At the time he already had 20 years of experience. He'd already made millions of dollars and lost a few too, and we were just getting started. **His experience became our experience, and he helped us take something that was already working for us and expand it. We already had a good solid foundation.**

It also helped that we had some business experience under our belts. When you're in business, you realize that there's no such thing as a perfect world. You have good days, you have bad days. Just like a good marriage, it goes through droughts, hills, and valleys, but you know you're committed. **People with business experience tend to do very, very well in this market — and not just because this market is so**

lucrative. You see, they're already used to the learning curve, and they realize that it's not a perfect world — that there's a price to pay for success. A lot of people who lack previous business experience just want everything handed to them, and they give up when the going gets tough. But a seasoned businessperson knows that there's no such thing as something for nothing, and they realize that if money is spent right, it's an investment towards future profits, not an expense.

> The gold is in your existing clients.
> — Joe Polish

There are two basic things here that can make you rich, and you need both. One is product knowledge: You've got to know everything about the product or service you're selling. This is so you can communicate it in the clearest way to all of your prospective customers and buyers, answer all their objections, and be 100% sold on it yourself. **The second thing is market knowledge: a real understanding of the people to whom you're trying to sell and resell. Of those two things, the most important is market knowledge.** The opportunity market can make you rich, because this market is so absolutely huge and so needy. **Millions of people desperately want to find a way to make more money but they don't know how.** They're scared, confused, and frustrated. There are rabid buyers out there spending all kinds of money looking for ways to make more money. **They're more than happy to spend huge sums of money.** We've had customers spend thousands and thousands of dollars with us on our various products and services. But that said, it's also a very skeptical marketplace, because there are so many scam artists out there in the opportunity market. Ironically, that's a great thing for you — because if you handle your business with complete honesty and integrity, you can win people over. **They'll be more than happy to continue to do business with you once you earn their trust.**

Another reason I love this marketplace is that there's an **endless array of products and services that you can create.** It never ends, and it's such a creative way to make money. **Another great thing about this market is that most of the competitors in it are very easy to beat.** Again, I don't mean to be disrespectful; that's just how it is. Now, I'm hoping that you, the reader, are going to get fired up about this market, get started in it, and make millions of dollars in it just like we have. I'm not worried about the competition; **I** *need* **competitors. We need more good people in this marketplace.** Since our company mails millions of pieces of direct-mail, if nothing else we need more companies that will put their lists up for rent — and I'm hoping to rent your list someday.

The more familiar you are with this market, the better; and when I started, I was very familiar with it. I knew that the competitors who were really kicking ass and taking names were few and far between; and they still are. **When you get right down to it, the competitors in this marketplace are very easy to beat, because there are so many fly-by-nighters out there.** These fly-by-night companies don't understand what real business is all about.

Another reason I love this marketplace is the fact that the best years are still to come, and it won't be long now. The Baby Boomer generation is just starting to retire. Now, what happens when people retire, after they play golf for six months and gain twenty or thirty pounds and watch too much TV, they start looking for something else to do. They find out that retirement isn't all that it's cracked up to be; in fact, it's terrible for most people. They have too much time on their hands; for years they've lived a structured life, where they've had a job to go to and they had people they worked with and things to do and places to go and people to see. Now they're retired, and the phone stops ringing. **The friends they worked with are busy doing the deal every day. This is one of the driving forces that causes people to start looking for business opportunities.**

A lot of those bored retirees are going to be taking a closer look at the opportunity market. **Millions of new people are going to be getting into this marketplace, year after year. Another thing about this marketplace is that it's very easy to get started in.** There are all kinds of ways to reach those millions of people who are desperately seeking a way to make more money, all kinds of magazines you can advertise in, plus direct-mail, card-packs, and the Internet. It's constantly evolving. **The millions of people in this marketplace share something in common, even though they're from different demographic groups. They all have that same insatiable desire to get rich.**

I'm the perfect example. Back when I first met my wife, when I was sending for all these plans and programs, I couldn't pay my bills. My electricity kept getting shut off. Why was that happening? Because I was using every last penny I had to buy all these get-rich-quick plans and programs. I was delusional — all my friends and family told me so. **It's true; I was obsessed.** A large percentage of the people who perpetually buy these plans and programs on a regular basis are overtaken with the same sense of delusion I had in the beginning. I don't mean to be judgmental about it; **I was an opportunity junkie for years. That's part of what makes this market so lucrative. These people are rabid buyers.**

Now, the way for you to get started is pretty simple, really. In fact, everything I have to share with you here is simple. Here is one example: **Start building a swipe file. Send away for all the different plans and programs that you can find — they're**

> **P**eople are much more *influenced* by the height of your *enthusiasm* than the depth of your knowledge.

everywhere. If you're not already on an opportunity mailing list, go to the nearest bookstore and find some opportunity magazines. Or go look in the back of *Popular Mechanics* or *Popular Science* — they've got great business opportunity sections. *USA Today* has a great biz-op section. Some of the most popular tabloids are good for business opportunity sellers, too. **Do this, and send away for fifty or a hundred programs. Pretty soon your name will be traded; it'll go out to all the different mailing lists, and it won't be long before your mailbox will be jam-packed, stuffed with different opportunity offers.** That's how you start building your swipe file — and then you have to start studying it.

When you start buying up these different moneymaking plans and programs, you'll see there's a lot of garbage in this market. **That should make you feel very confident.** Remember, the competitors in this market are very easy to beat.

This is the last point I'm going to make before we go on: **I want you to think carefully about all the unhappiness in this marketplace. You see, that's what causes people to buy.** There are a lot of people who are frustrated when it comes to money. They want to get rich, they want to make more money, they're desperately seeking a way to do it; **but they're so frustrated, and they're so confused. They're even desperate.** A lot of them are fearful; they know that the window is closing. They know that they only have a couple of good decades left in them, and they're desperately searching for a way to make more money. Plus, they want some excitement. **There are all these emotional factors,** and I've already talked about one of the biggest ones, which nobody else will tell you about — the sense of delusion in this market.

There are millions of people like me who have never made any money. That's the way I was in the 1980s, just barely getting by, but spending every last dollar. In some cases, I was even saving it up. If I found a good plan or program I wanted, I'd save all my money for six or eight weeks, until I had a couple of thousand dollars, and I would spend it all at once. **So don't think that just because a lot of people in this marketplace are broke right now that they can't get their hands on hundreds or even thousands of dollars.** Because they can save it up, and they're willing to spend it once they do. **It's a rabid marketplace.** The marketplace is driven by emotional factors; the obsessions that people have, the insatiability. These folks are driven by a strong, overwhelming desire to make more money. **They dream of getting rich.** It's what they think of from the minute they get up to the minute they go to bed at night. As a result, there's a small group of people — I'm one of them — who are making millions and millions of dollars in this marketplace. You can be one of them too, and this secret is so vitally important for you. **It's just to become familiar with the marketplace.**

So consider carefully about what I've said here; break it down and think about it. **The opportunity market really can make you rich, and I'd like for you to start thinking carefully about this marketplace and start buying some of the available opportunities, and start building and studying your swipe file.**

CHAPTER

7

Selling is finding out what people want, and then letting them have

When people start thinking about what they want to sell, or they realize they want to get in business and make money, they tend to start by coming up with an idea for a product or a service — and then they try to find a market of people who want that product or service. But starting with a product or service is the wrong way to go about it: in fact, it's exactly backwards. You have to start by finding a market, and then flip it around and find a service that that market wants. Even then, even if you think you've found a market or you know there's a market out there for your product or service, that market may be too small. You may not be able to make any long-term profits off that market. **Since long-term profits are your goal, the way to achieve them is to find a large, starving market with a large amount of discretionary income.** The bigger the market, the more money you can make with that product or service. Let's put it more plainly: to do well in marketing, no matter the product, you have to find out exactly what people (or more specifically, a group of people) really want, and then let them have it.

The opportunity market is a perfect example. There are millions of people who want to stay home and make more money. Same with the diet market: millions want to lose weight. In the sweepstakes market, there are millions who want to win prizes and money. I could go on and on, but I think you get the point — **your best bet is to <u>start</u> <u>with</u> <u>a</u> <u>group</u> <u>of</u> <u>people</u> <u>with</u> <u>a</u> <u>common</u> <u>bond</u> <u>or</u> <u>interest</u>, and work your product backwards from there to cater to that market.** That's not being cynical, that's reality.

Because I'm in the opportunity market and it's something I'm familiar with and study a lot, that's what I'm going to focus on here. Like I said earlier, there are millions of people who want to make money from home. **They're not lazy: they just want to work for themselves.** They've tried working for "the man," and know there's no future in it. That market wants useful, proven information products they can use to prosper and earn a living. When you start by focusing on that market, you can find something in particular they're looking for and develop products and services to match what they want.

Speaking of wanting, I want to make one brief distinction between what people want and what people need. Usually they're different: sometimes the two can go hand-in-hand, but often they don't. So don't focus on developing products and services that the market needs — instead, spend your time developing products that the market wants, and more likely than not you'll have a lot easier time making money. That's where the real money is. **People often spend twice as much money on something they want than on something they need.**

A "want" is an unfulfilled desire. <u>That</u> <u>unfulfilled</u> <u>desire</u> <u>creates</u> <u>the</u> <u>vacuum</u> <u>for</u> <u>the</u> <u>product</u> <u>or</u> <u>service</u> <u>you</u> <u>want</u> <u>to</u> <u>sell</u>. It helps to visualize the situation, as my friend and colleague Jeff Gardner likes to point out. Let's say you have a group of people out in the middle of the Sahara Desert, and they've been out

> The pain of discipline hurts less than the pain of regret.

there for days and days. They're all sweating to death, and they don't have any water. Ultimately, they all know they're going to die — and the only thing they really have in their pockets is cash. Say you come along with one canteen of water. How many people are going to pony-up money because they want that water? You may say, "Okay, they need that water," and if you're any kind of human being you'll give it to them for free.

That was kind of an extreme example — very few wants are life-or-death needs. But here's how you have to look at it: **there are markets of people who are just as thirsty for products they want** as for those people in the Sahara Desert would be for a glass of water. If you go out there and you find the markets with that kind of a drive and a passion for something that they want — something they crave and have an unfulfilled desire for — you don't have to worry about coming up with product ideas because the market will tell you what they want, and what they're willing to pay for it. It's a very simple system, but it is making many people super rich! **It's not about going out and trying to find products and develop products, but finding that key want or need, and then to find a way to fill it.**

A friend of mine says something that's a little controversial, but it illustrates his point well: he says he wants to sell donuts to fat people. He wants to sell heroin to drug addicts. He wants to sell porno to sex fiends. Sure, these examples are metaphorical, he's not going to do anything illegal or immoral to make money by preying on people's addictions, and he's not suggesting that you do so, <u>but you should look for markets with that kind of hunger</u>. Find the people who are already hungry, who just can't wait to give you the money for what they want or need. He's also saying to make it simple on yourself. **Go where the market is — don't try to create one where it isn't.** Don't try to sell heroin to people as they're coming out of the church, go down to the seedy sides of town.

In short, my friend is saying that you should find the market first, and then serve it. That's important because too many people fall in love with a product or service, and they want to try to sell it to everyone, the market be damned. But let me make this point again: **you must find the market first and then serve the market.** Some of the best Direct-Mail millionaires I know <u>based their products on existing products that they or someone else were already selling</u>. Let's say they find a certain book that sold 75,000 copies by Direct-Mail; they study that book and write a manual or book or CD that's is similar to that, and they sell their version. **People are insatiable!** If a person is a horseracing fan, they're going to buy more than one or two gambling books on horse racing. If they want to make money, they keep buying moneymaking products. To use the porno illustration: the person who has two or three porno magazines or videos is the best candidate to buy a hundred more. **It's a very sound marketing principle that can make you huge, never-ending profits!**

CHAPTER

8

Constant Testing. What's Next?

We used this secret to make millions of dollars: We tested as many different things as we could. We're always asking ourselves, "What's next?" It's not work in the traditional way that most people think of work; this is more like a game. It's more like a hobby, an activity that you do for total enjoyment. **Work really does mix with pleasure if you do it the right way; you'll enjoy what you're doing and you'll make a lot more money.** The secret is to treat work as if it were a game. What you're doing is searching for the ultimate way to make millions of dollars, and if you'll do that, you'll have a lot more fun; it won't just seem like work, and even the things that are difficult will become easier because you're totally focused on finding those one or two ideas. You can make a lot of money if you'll do this. It's simpler and easier than you can ever imagine. You'll see that it's just the way of life for you. **It's about serving your customers in the highest possible way, and then going out there to new prospects and offering them the same types of things you offered to your best customers.**

The secret to earning the biggest profit is just to stay focused on your best customers. Who are they? What do they want the most? What do they *buy* the most? The better you're able to answer those questions, the more money you'll make. That comes with experience and knowledge; it doesn't happen overnight, and the ideas you get today aren't going to be nearly as good as the ideas you'll get tomorrow. Sometimes it takes months or years to intimately know your customer. **But once you do, you've got the golden key in your hand to making millions of dollars, and that's a great feeling.** It's more than just the money and all the material things you're going to buy. That stuff is nice, but it has its limits. Money's a great thing to have, but you can only sleep in one bed at a time, eat one meal at a time, live in one home at a time, drive one great car at a time.

There's only so much joy and satisfaction that comes from money, and you need to get that out of your system. **The joy is in the acquisition of it all; it's in the hunt, it's in the chase. That's what's going to give you the greatest pleasure when it comes to getting rich.** It's looking for those ideas that are going to be your next golden winners. **I think about it as a metaphor of a huge bank vault:** we don't know what the combination is, so we're safecrackers in this metaphor. We're searching for that combination. We've got our stethoscope pressed against that two-foot-thick steel door. All the money we'll ever want and need is on the other side of that door, and so we're carefully trying different combinations, looking for just the right combination to cause the tumblers in that safe to come into complete alignment so the door will swing open and all that money is ours. **I think about that often when we're testing new ideas;** and you really do need to have that whole sporting attitude going, because when you find what works the best, when you have a promotion that's working and all of a sudden hundreds of thousands — and in some cases millions — of dollars are flowing in in a very short period of time, that's great fun; and that's the part I want you to focus on. **It's nice to have all that money, but what's even nicer, and what will give you the most satisfaction, is knowing that you have the ability within yourself to create it anytime you want to.** Anytime you want to make another fortune, you know exactly how to get it. **The key is to go to your best customers first. Stay totally focused on them, and start testing from what I call the top down.** Every new idea is tested to your very best customers first. Those are the people who know you, respect you, and trust you; and because of that, the selling resistance is lowered.

A few years back, we got involved in an interesting opportunity. This guy came to me with an outrageous idea; it almost sounded like some scam. He came at me with, "Hey, T.J., if I said I had a proven way to make $750,000 to $1 million this year and all you had to

> **B**low your own horn! Nobody's going to blow your horn for you — you gotta get out there and do it!

do was a work a little to get it, would you be interested?" If anybody else had said that to me, I would have said, "No thank you," or I would have sent them to one of my staff members. But because this is a guy I've known for a few years, and he's somebody I want to continue to do business with. Because I trust him and I like him, I was open and receptive. I want you to think about that. **Your best customers will buy almost anything from you, especially if they know they can get their money back if they're not happy.** Those are the people you should approach first; it's what I call your "warm market." And then, of course, you have other groups of customers within your customer base, because of the way that you pre-qualify them.

You can (and should) segment your customer base by the amount of money they spend, or how recently they spent things — because sometimes people get into emotional heat for a certain type of product or service. While they're in that mindset, you'd better sell them everything you can, because you never know when they're going to settle down. **So you segment, sometimes by the frequency of their purchase; you know they're excited about your type of offer.** You know that they're hot for it. You've got to use that knowledge to go after them in a more aggressive way than you would the rest of your customers. **Or, you segment them by what it is they bought from you the first time.** Remember the general answer to the question: "What do people want?" That's where a lot of marketers are confused. They run around in total bewilderment, thinking, "I don't know what to sell!" The answer is to sell people variations on the theme of whatever you sold them the first time. It's really very simple. When you look at everything in a holistic way and examine it from the top down instead of the bottom up, it becomes easier to figure out what's going to make you the most amount of money.

First of all, stay totally focused on your very best customers. Forget about all of those other people out there, and do what you have to do to make profits in the first place — which is serve your customers. **Do very special things for them and create all kinds of opportunities for them, because you're using them as a testing ground; but you're also doing everything possible to serve them in the highest way, and to look for the things that excite them the most.** You want more people like your best customers. That's the whole goal of your marketing. **You want to attract the very best people and repel the worst people.** I always run into these great customers at my seminars, and I know their buying history; I know that they've been with us for years, and they've spent thousands and thousands of dollars. Sometimes I'm able to build enough of a rapport with them enough where I'm able to ask them face-to-face, "Where do I find another thousand just like you?" If I don't have enough rapport built with them, I at least think it. That's the question you should be asking too.

You're looking for people who will spend a huge sum of money with you over a long period of time, because they have such a deep interest in what you're selling. It causes them to buy and rebuy because they trust you and like you, you've built a real rapport with them, and you've expressed yourself enough to them where they know that you care for them. Your best customers will forgive you for not being perfect, because they know you're striving to reach out to them, to give them more of what they want the most. You end up knowing your best customers better than they know themselves.

For years I kept journals, and every time I learned something new about a customer, I would write it down. Those journals got filled with all kinds of things, and we had testimonial sheets that went out disguised as surveys. **We would reward the customer with a free bonus if they filled out a survey and sent it back to us.** They'd give us permission to use their comments in any way we wanted to, and we'd give them a free gift. Well, I had those transcribed, and I saved all the best ones. Sometimes people just wanted to fill out the bare minimum so they could get the free gift, but about one out of three was really good. **I transcribed them and took notes and did a lot of careful thinking, until I got to the place where I am today, which is a high level of confidence that I understand my**

customers better than they understand themselves. I know why they buy. **Ninety percent of the time, it's for emotional reasons.** I've also done a lot of heavy reflection on all of the reasons that I personally used to buy those moneymaking programs, because that was our entry into the marketplace.

Little did we know it at the time, but we had a lot of insider knowledge — because I was buying them all. **I was obsessed with buying the same kinds of plans and programs that we sell now, and when I say obsessed, I mean it.** Now, succeeding with most of these plans involves a lot of work — unfortunately or fortunately. It's unfortunate because people want to delude themselves that they can make millions of dollars with no effort. It's a fantasy. It's what I call lottery mentality: you just know you're going to buy a ticket and win the grand prize. The fortunate part for you is that because there's a good bit of time, work and effort involved in succeeding with these programs, **it levels the playing field.** The desire to make millions of dollars is the most important thing, because through that desire, you'll hopefully be willing to do whatever it takes — and there are a lot of people who aren't. **The good news is, yes, all this *does* take some time, work, and effort to learn; but if you're willing to go through what you must and do whatever it takes, then you're going to be part of a small minority.** This makes it all that much easier for you.

> The "perception" that you always have something "new" and exciting to share with them is one of the things that will *always* keep them coming back for more!

People are looking for a simple, easy way to make millions of dollars. That way does exist, but *only* after you develop these skills. Then it becomes quite easy. When we first met Russ von

Hoelscher, one of the first things he said to us was vital. I'll never forget; we'd known him for a little while by then, and had talked on the phone a bunch of times. He's a likeable, friendly guy who really does care about other people, and he had more than 20 years of experience at the time. In the course of a conversation as I was driving him home from the airport one day, he said the words that stuck in my mind and have dominated my thoughts ever since. He said, **"All it really takes to make millions of dollars in this business is just one idea."** I just about drove the car off the road, I was so excited. I was so thrilled at that, and I still am, and since then we've proven it to be true. It's not just some concept that I'm throwing out because it sounds good. It's true. All you need is just one idea. **That's one of the reasons why you should continue to experiment with as many new ideas as possible, so you can find that one idea.** Or it may be some combination of ideas, because **sometimes the ideas that make you the most money are the ones you mix together with other things you've tried.** That's been a large part of the secret to our success. You continue to find new ways to mix different ideas together.

Often the secret you're looking for is a combination of other things that have worked for you in the past. **One of things we do is continue to find new ways to repackage the same, successful ideas that have already made us huge sums of money.** Why not? You're there to serve your customers. You're there to give them more of what they bought from you before. Now, customers always want new stuff. New, new, new; everybody loves it. It's part of our thinking. **If you don't offer your customers new stuff, someone else will.** Either you get the money, or one of your competitors gets the money.

You've got to do it, if for no other reason than that you

recognize and accept the fact that marketing is about attracting and re-attracting customers, retaining customers, continuing to do business with the same people again and again — as long as your customers don't get the idea that you're just trying to slam them all the time. No matter what you do, some customers are always going to feel you're just trying to take advantage of them, that you're just trying to get their money. **So your messages have to be altruistic, and you really must have a desire to serve the customers and offer strong money-back guarantees.** Let your customers know that if they're ever unhappy, they can get their money back. That way, you're dealing with a lot of integrity.

The second reason you have to continue to test new ideas all the time is because you never know where your next multimillion-dollar idea is going to come from. **Your biggest breakthrough could be right around the corner, and unless you're testing new ideas you're never going to find it.** Make a game of it; have fun with it. **The next reason to test is that the secret to getting great ideas is to get *many* ideas.** More ideas lead to better ideas, and the more things you test, the more power you'll have. **The very best, most profitable ideas are often a combination of many ideas — the themes, formats, and models that you've used before.** The best ideas for you will often be a combination of many different things that you've done, the years that you've spent intimately getting to know who your customers are, what they want the most and why they continue to rebuy, and how to give those things to them.

Your biggest breakthrough is out there right now. One idea really does lead to another. It's an evolutionary process, and your biggest breakthroughs will be a new combination of different ideas that you've used before. **The more ideas you test,**

Blur the lines between <u>work</u> and <u>play</u>.

the more wealth-making power you have. Again, it's all about selling to your very best customers, because you're doing what I call testing from the top down instead of the bottom up. You're constantly thinking about that smaller group of people who buy and rebuy from you the most. **I recommend that you have seminars and workshops just so you can get face-to-face with these customers.**

Too many direct response marketers, especially this new breed of Internet marketers out there, **want to hide out from the customers. They're attracted to direct response marketing because they don't want to be face-to-face with people.** One of things that really turned me on the most about this business in the beginning was that I could do everything from home. I was in love with the idea that I could do business with hundreds, thousands, even hundreds of thousands of people without ever meeting most of them. **But you can't really hide out from your best customers.** If for no other reason than that, have seminars constantly so that you can get up-close and personal with them. You can get to know them that way. **The most rabid markets out there, the ones where you can make the largest amount of money in the fastest period, are 100% emotional driven.**

You also have to think conceptually. See the absolute simplicity of even the most complicated ideas; find the hidden secrets behind the ideas that are making other people money right now. See it simpler, believe it bigger. **Go to your best customers first, and then test through the rest of your customer base.** Take the ideas that make you the most money and use them for new acquisitions. **It's the most risk-free way to make money.**

I also recommend that you schedule meetings on a regular basis. We've been having regular weekly meetings now for well over ten years. **We're always asking ourselves what's next, and we're planning different mailings, and we number all of them, and we schedule them, and we make commitments to do new things before we have all the answers figured out.** Remember, your best customers will gladly buy almost an unlimited number of products and services from you. I used to worry that I was trying to sell to my best customers way too often, and I was always afraid that those customers were going to leave me; and what I found is that nothing could be further from the truth. **They're going to buy and rebuy from other companies unless I'm selling to them.** Now I just worry whether I'm selling enough to them, and I'm trying to stay out there in front of my best customers all the time, offering them other products and services.

You'll do well as long as the products and services you're offering help them get more of what you know they want, as long as you're striving to serve them in the highest way, as long as you're not just trying to suck money out of people for no value. You're trying to offer value for value; actually, you're trying to offer greater value than what you're getting. **So you're giving them more and more of what you know that they want.** As long as you're providing tremendous value and running your business in an ethical way — where they can get their money back without any game-playing, if they want it — you'll build their trust, and they'll end up buying more stuff from you.

Then, last but not least, keep finding new ways to recycle and repackage the same products and services; the same models that you tried before, the same ideas, the same themes, everything that's worked great for you in the past.

Keep trying to find new ways to give products a facelift, a new theme. **Try to come up with something that looks new but is actually just repackaged; and again, the more you do it, the easier it'll get.** People love new stuff, and they want new stuff; but if it's too new, it won't fly. Nobody wants to be the guinea pig; and so what you do is find new stuff for your customers. But then you let them know that it's not *entirely* new. **It's still based on something that's solid and proven and tested, and there's still that conservative element present; because if it's too new, people are going to freak out.** If it's too new, it will arouse their skepticism. So you're constantly coming out with variations on a theme. The car companies do it all the time. The best movies are just variations on a theme of all the other best movies. People want proven models, again and again.

This is a secret that most markets never put enough time and effort into. They'll never go through the painful learning curve of testing new things and working all this out. **But if you'll do it, you'll become part of a small group that's making huge amounts of money.**

CHAPTER

9

Develop Your Copywriting Skills

The secret that made us millions of dollars is the fact that we learned how to write copy that sells, and then how to implement it in our overall marketing strategy. Now, this is arguably the single greatest wealth-making skill you can learn. Knowing you can write a sales letter that causes thousands of people to give you millions of dollars is one of the greatest feelings on earth. I want you to experience this feeling. It's just an amazing thing: to get an idea, write a sales letter, send it out to your best customers — and if you have enough of those customers, you can make millions of dollars. Maybe there are greater feelings than that, but this is one of the top five you could ever experience.

So many people want to make millions of dollars... and they could, if only they'd just realize how simple it is to do it! **You've got to have a group of customers who respect you, who feel great about you and who know you're out there to help them; and you've got to have the ability to communicate to them, simply by sending them a sales letter or a series of sales**

letters. You see, that's what it's really about. One sales letter can make you millions of dollars, but the key is having a group of customers that you can send a series of sales letters to on a regular basis, so you build a business, not just a promotion. That's what you're really after: a business, which is steady profits made over a period of time. That's the key to overall profitability.

Now, what is a great sales letter? **A great sales letter is something that replaces a live salesperson.** So if you have a thousand sales letters out there, you have a thousand sales people. **It's a salesperson in an envelope. It does a complete job of selling for you.** It answers every objection in the minds and hearts of the skeptical prospect, and the fearful prospect, and the prospect who feels overwhelmed. They're already getting a lot of solicitations, because the same people that are your best customers are also other peoples' best customers. **Your sales letter answers all their objections, and it stands out from all of the other mail. It's interesting to read, it's targeted to a specific person, it establishes the value of whatever you're selling, and it proves to them that what you have to offer is worth far more than the money you're asking for in exchange.** It makes people excited about giving you their money. That's what a great sales letter is. It's exciting, it's interesting, and it's persuasive.

It's the ultimate way for you to stay in touch with your customers and to continue to resell to them on a regular basis, to give them more of what you know they want the most. **It's also the fastest way for you to make the largest amount of money.** They don't call it direct-mail for no reason. This is a media that goes straight to the prospect or customer, and it delivers a very direct sales presentation to them. It compels them to send their money directly to you, and it's the fastest way for you to make millions of dollars. **Direct-mail is a media that you have 100% control over, from start to finish.** You write it; you design it; you choose your printer. You choose the mailing house that's going to mail out your sale letter; you schedule it; you pick all of the mailing lists; you analyze the numbers as they come in. You have total control and total power over every aspect of this. It's a media that you own, and that's the way I want you to think about direct-mail.

Think about it as if you had your own TV station — or better still, think about it as if you had your own newspaper, and you control every aspect of that newspaper. You have regular subscribers who get it, and your job is to make sure that those subscribers stay subscribers. But

> **Y**our goal for each day is to come up with at <u>least</u> <u>one</u> <u>new</u> <u>idea</u> that you *didn't* have yesterday for increasing your sales and profits!

even better, when you have direct-mail, your job is also to advertise in your own newspaper, and your job is to make sure that the largest number of your subscribers continue to give you money for all the advertising in your newspaper. It's a great metaphor; it'll help you think about this in the right way. Let's say you own your own newspaper, which you publish on a regular basis. It's a job; you just do it, and you send it out there on a regular basis to people that you know want it, because they subscribe. That's really what we're trying to explain here. **This is a media that you control. You call all the shots. You have all the power; you have all of the freedom and flexibility to do whatever it is that you want to do with it.**

That's the kind of control you don't have in other kinds of media, where you're totally dependent on the publication itself. They're the ones who set the deadlines; they're the ones to set the prices. If you want lower prices you have to negotiate, and it's often a painful thing. You're not in any position of power. But when you have a group of customers who have bought from you in the past, you know what they like and you know what they don't like; there's a trust that's built up between you and them. **You can mail to them as often as you want, and you control exactly what you want them to see, every aspect of it; you're in charge.** You don't have to ask permission from anybody. If you're not happy with the printers or the mailing house you're using, you can find new ones. If you're not happy with the mailing list broker, you can go out and find somebody else. You can mail as often as you want, as much as you want. If you've got a piece that's working and you know that there are more names out there, all you have to do is call your mailing list broker and say, "Hey! Give me another 50,000 names!" and then call your printer and say, "Print up another 50,000 pieces!" Then you call your mailing house and say, "Hey! We're going to mail another 50,000 pieces!" It's as simple as that.

You control it all, and it's a no-risk method if you use it correctly. Here's what I mean by that: **You're constantly using direct-mail to test new ideas — and you can test *radical* new ideas, ideas that are totally bold and audacious.** You can test them to small groups of your best customers first, and because the trust is established with those people, chances are they'll buy from you. You're looking for the things that make them most excited, the things that they buy the most. **You'll never lose money, because these are people who will, in most cases, buy anything from you if you've done your job right.** Then you take the things they buy the most of, the ones they're most excited about, and start testing them to other groups of customers. Then, if your numbers are still high, you start testing to outside mailing lists, the lists of prospects your customers all originated from. There are companies in your marketplace that sell the same types of products and services that you sell. If you're in a direct response marketing-friendly environment, those companies will be putting their mailing lists up for rent. **At M.O.R.E., Inc., we rent our mailing lists out to all kinds of other companies.** Our mailing-list manager picks the ones he wants; we're only renting our list out to companies he knows are honorable ones. **Similarly, we rent names from other companies who have their mailing lists up for rent.**

That's the way it is with the opportunity market; millions of names every year are available. **These are proven buyers, folks who have bought other moneymaking plans and programs just like the ones we offer, so there's a buying history.** We can go to the people we know are interested in what we sell, and we can offer them the kinds of programs that we sell to bring them into the fold; and now they become our customers. There are plenty of markets out there just like the opportunity market, where you can rent, in some cases, millions of names every year.

The big secret is that, by the time we get to the point of sending an offer to those outside names, we've already tested the product to our very small group of best customers. Think of your customer base as a pyramid: it gets smaller as it goes up. We test to the very best of our customers at the top of the pyramid. We take the offers that work the best there, the ones that produce the most sales and profits, and we slowly start testing to larger groups of customers, working our way down from there. Then, when we go through our entire customer base and the offer's still good, we take that offer and we start testing it to the outside mailing list. **By the time we use it for our new customer acquisition, it's proven. We know it works.** The only question now is, how well is it going to work with people who don't already have a relationship with us?

I just love direct-mail. Direct-mail and the ability to write copy: together, they're such a powerful thing. It's absorbing; it's interesting. You can spend hour after hour absorbed in this, and it becomes more a hobby or an art than anything else. That's the way I think about it. Sure, it's work; it's a lot of work. This is, again, one of the great things about it. I don't say this to dissuade or discourage you; I just want to say that it's taken me a lot of time and work to master my skills at writing copy that sells millions of dollars worth of products and services. **To some extent it's been a labor of love, but in a whole other way it's just been an awful lot of work.** There are parts that are more interesting than others. Some parts are very relaxing. Every night my wife and I sit on the couch, and I'm half-watching TV programs with her; but the other half of me is quietly editing sales copy I've already written. To me, that's the most relaxing way to spend an evening.

I'm always working on different sales letters, constantly. I always have different projects out there, and it's the most wonderful feeling to create these things that produce revenue.

> The true secret of success is to be <u>bold</u> and <u>tenacious</u>!

produce revenue. It's almost like alchemy. If you study history, you'll see that up until about the sixteenth or seventeenth century, there were people called alchemists, and their job was to try to turn lead into gold — to try to take something of no value, basically, and turn it into high value. That's what we're doing here. The copywriters like myself, who know how to design and develop and create sales letters that cause thousands of people to willingly and gladly give their money to us — **well, we're taking paper and ink, which has very little value, and making it high value.** Of course you can do it on websites too, but basically it's the same thing concept. **You're creating a complete sales story from top to bottom, and you're causing people to get so excited that they just can't wait to give you their money.** We've had people wire their money to us through Western Union just to get our product quicker. We've had many people who Federal Expressed their orders to us. A few have jumped in their cars and driven from three or four states away, because they wanted to get the product even faster.

It's exciting to create millions of dollars worth of revenue where no revenue existed before, and to know that you're the one who did it. Now, I've had a lot of help over the years, learning how to write copy; and **the best thing I can do is tell you that you have to just decide that you want to become a great copywriter.** Make that decision. For years, I could write sales letters to my best customers. They trusted me; we had established relationships, and quite candidly my copy didn't have to be as good because of the relationship. It's just like when you have a friend — you'll do more for your friend. **If you have two people who ask you to do something and one of them is your friend, you're going to go with your friend every time.** Your friend hardly has to say anything. They just say, "Look, I've got this great deal," and you say "Hey! Stop, stop, I trust you. How much is it going to cost me?" Whereas any other person is going to have to work on you quite a bit. They're going to have to keep bugging you, over and over again.

If you just think about it like that, you'll realize that when you have an established group of customers, you don't have to be as good. **Even a beginning copywriter can start sharpening their skills, creating new offers, writing new sales letters to those people who have shown a certain level of trust because they bought from you the first time.** So for years, I would write these sales letters to our established customers. This is how I developed my skills as a copywriter. **It was just to write sales letters to people who had already bought from us. They knew us; they liked us.** There was some trust there, shown by the money they had given us. People vote with their checkbooks or their credit cards, and so for years I crafted all of these offers that went out to people who had already bought from us, and it was great to learn how to write copy and send it out there to people. When we wrote "Dear Friend," we really meant it. We were trying to be friends with our customers; we were trying to befriend them in every way, and that's what I'm asking you to do, too. **Operate with complete integrity and complete honesty.** Treat your customers very well and make all kinds of offers to them, and then take the best of those offers and use them for your new customer acquisition program. **There are plenty of mailing lists out there, but only the very best offers and the very best sales copy will work for those people who don't know you.** They don't trust you yet; they're still very skeptical. You're just another company showing up in their mailbox now.

For years I tried to write copy for new customer acquisition, and I simply couldn't do it; I wasn't good enough. That used to just tick me off! I used to get so angry because I was dependent on outside copywriters, and I wanted to learn how to do it myself. That anger and frustration emerged every single time we were forced to hire a copywriter because my copy wasn't good enough. I would take sales letters or variations that had worked great for our customers, and I tried to make them work to the outside list, and the profits were just never there. **Then these outside copywriters came in who had a limited amount of knowledge and understanding of what we were selling and who we were selling it to — and**

yet they could go out there and make the copy work.

That just made me so angry — and I used that anger in a positive way. **I became determined that I was going to be able to do this. I studied a lot of sales letters, I read a lot of books, I practiced a lot.** This is one suggestion from Gary Halbert — arguably one of the best copywriters ever: a true legend according to many, including me. **Gary said that the way to learn how to write copy is to take one of the best ads you can find, the long-form, full-page ads, or one of the best sales letters, and to write it longhand word for word, over and over, until you get so sick and tired of it you can't stand it anymore.**

No matter how bad your business may be right now — as long as you have a huge list of customers — you are always only one irresistible offer away from making bazillions of dollars!

I did that; I took the *Lazy Man's Way to Riches*, a full-page ad that Joe Carbo used in the mid-1970s that made him millions and millions of dollars, and rewrote it in my own hand, day after day. I don't know how long I did it; at least for a couple of months, to the point where I just about had the whole thing memorized. **I learned the language, the rhythm, the flow of writing good, persuasive, hard-hitting sales copy.** That particular ad caused so many people to get excited that they sent in their money; and subconsciously, over a period of time, with the determination that I was going to learn how to write sales copy that really was capable of making millions of dollars, **I became a good copywriter. It wasn't easy; it's still not easy.** It's painful work at times, and don't let anybody kid you. There's a quote that I love: it says, **"The secret of great writing is to re-write,"** and I'm famous for re-writing my sales letters a

whole bunch of times. That's what I'm doing on the couch every single night.

So I want you to think about that tonight; think about me tonight. Whatever you're doing tonight, realize that if it's before ten-thirty in the evening Central Time, **I'm on my couch next to my lovely wife Eileen, I've got a laptop in my lap, and I'm re-writing some sales letter. When I get up in the morning, I work on the copy. I work on sales letters all the time.** I've always got about three or four of them going at once, because I get bored with them, and I want to keep shifting around. It's more like a job now than anything, but still there's moments when this is just the most wonderful feeling on Earth, and **one of my secrets is, whenever I get really excited about an idea, I just start writing like crazy.** Some of the sales letters that have worked the best have been those I wrote when I was higher than a kite on caffeine. I tend to drink a pot of coffee or two every day. So I get wound up, I get excited about ideas. **The time to write copy is when you're in the heat of the moment, when you're really pumped up and excited.** Now, that can change; over a period of time, your skill and knowledge will develop to the point where you can write powerful, persuasive copy whether you're excited or not. You can still make it look like you're excited, and that's the method used by freelance copywriters who charge many thousands of dollars. They don't really understand what your products are and who you're selling to, but they can create copy that's compelling. It looks like they were excited when they wrote it, when the truth is that they hardly understand anything about it.

This is a skill that can set you up for life. It's your meal ticket; it's the way to riches; it's the single greatest wealth building skill that you'll ever learn, when you think about the

overall picture. That's what I want you to do: think beyond just writing one sales letter or whatever. **Think about copywriting as a lifelong skill you can use to sell and resell to your customers again and again, and to attract new customers to you.** Remember: the secret is to take your best promotions, work them through your customer base first, then send them out as part of your new customer acquisition process. That'll save you a lot of misery, because **if your existing customers aren't excited, then you know that the people out there who don't know you won't be excited.** There's no differentiation in their mind between you and all the other direct-mail they're getting.

These are the brutal realities we're dealing with here. **There's a lot of competition, and people are sorting their mail over the trash can.** When it comes to front-end, new customer acquisition, it's really tough to break through that shell of skepticism. But when you're mailing to existing customers, it's so much easier. You should have new offers going out to them all the time.

We've been doing this since 1988, and I used to worry that I was sending too much too often to our established customers. I don't worry about that anymore, and I don't think you should either. **As long as you're making great offers that are altruistic in nature, that really offer tremendous value, that offer strong money-back guarantees if people aren't happy; that strive to give your customers special deals — then you're good.** The perception is that other people aren't getting these things; you're offer's just for them. **You should be in their mailbox constantly.** The beautiful thing about it is, if you structure it right, and if your customer base is large enough, you don't need very many people to respond to an offer to make millions of dollars. **The secret of making your customer base** large enough is to have a steady stream of mail that goes out on a regular basis to attract new customers to you, so your customer base continues to grow bigger automatically.

Problems and pain ARE GOOD THINGS! Competitive people see problems and pain as challenges. They use the pressure of adversity to spur them on to new heights!

We have one direct-mail offer out there all the time to new customers. Every single week, 52 weeks a year now; we used to stop around Christmas time, but we don't anymore. **Fifty-two weeks of every year, we extend tens of thousands of direct-mail solicitations to new customers who have never done business with us before.** We want to get them to buy once, or get them to take some minor action, so we can bring them into the fold. Nowadays, I'm way beyond that fear that I had for years, the fear that I would tick off my customers if I sent them too many offers. **I realize now that I literally lost millions of dollars because I didn't market aggressively to our established customers,** because I was always holding back, always afraid that we were doing too much to those customers. **Now, we strive to have one new offer that goes out there to our established customers every single week. That's our goal.** We don't hit it every week, but we try to, so we're in their mailbox 52 times a year. **To make a profit on most promotions, we only need a small percentage of people to raise their hands and say "Yes."**

The same can be true of your promotions, if you structure them correctly. **You can make millions of dollars, and you'll always make more money by mailing more often to your very best customers.**

CHAPTER

10

The Six-Step Million-Dollar Sales Letter Formula

In this chapter, I'll introduce you to the Six-Step Million-Dollar Sales Letter Formula! **These are the six steps that you can use to write a sales letter that can make you millions of dollars.** Now, can I promise you that you *will* make millions of dollars? Absolutely not! Anybody who makes you a promise like that is lying to you.

But what I *will* promise you is that this same exact six-step formula has made us millions of dollars here at M.O.R.E., Inc. **We use this formula (or a variation thereof) on a regular basis.** We learned it from studying other sales letters by master copywriters—from doing just what I told you to do in the last chapter. **We broke down the sales letters that were making other people multimillionaires, derived this simple formula, and used the heck out of it.** It's a formula that you can use, too. **As you'll see, it can work for almost any product or service.** I'll admit that the formula works better for some products and services than it works for others; but if you'll carefully consider these six steps, **you'll realize that**

copywriting really is very simple and formulaic. It's just a set of processes that you go through.

All this will help you get on the other side of the cash register. **The more you do that, the more you'll see commonalities in how these steps are used.** That will take the mystery out of it, and will empower you to write your own sales copy. Hopefully, it will give you great confidence, so you can develop your own sales material that can, in fact, make you millions of dollars. The money's out there, in the pockets, purses, and lines of credit of tens of millions of Americans, let alone the people from other countries whom you can easily do business with nowadays. **There are *billions* of people looking for all kinds of products and services.** You can use formulas just like the one I'll tell you here to offer people such useful things that they'll gladly give you their money!

I love talking about marketing, and copywriting specifically, because it's such a vital part of the Direct Response business. Some people might try to tell you, "Ah, you don't need to know how to write sales copy." **But I think that if you're serious about being a Direct Response Marketer, you *must* learn how to write good copy.** It's one thing to have someone else write a sales letter for you once, or to use an outsourced copywriter occasionally; **But if you don't know how to write your own sales copy, you have a severe disadvantage compared with someone else who does.**

So learning how to be a good copywriter is vital if you're serious about being in the Direct Response business... or really, in my estimation, being in any business. I think that every business out there—no matter what it is, no matter whether it's online or offline, no matter whether it's someone working out of a spare bedroom in their house or they've got a retail storefront selling on Main Street, U.S.A.—can benefit from DRM. **Every business can benefit by having its owner or its Marketing Director learn how to write good sales copy.**

We have 6 steps in our formula; other people may be using the same basics in writing their sales copy, but maybe they've got it down to a 5-step formula, or possibly their formula is 10 steps. You could probably expand or shrink this concept to fit whatever model you want. But the basics are here. **These six steps can help you write killer sales letters that can bring cash into your mailbox, into your e-mail box, over the phone, or however you take orders.**

Early on, Russ von Hoelscher—the man who helped us make millions of dollars initially—told us that **all it takes is one good sales letter to make a million dollars.** We've had quite a few do that for us! And then, of course, **we tend to rewrite the same sales letters over and over again, so we've had many sales letters that have generated more than a million over the years.** That's not to brag; certainly other people have made our success look pale by comparison. It's just to show that this really does work!

---

treet-smart business rule: **Take good care of the people who are taking good care of you!** Surround yourself with the best people you can find. Then don't run them off!

The FIRST STEP is this: You've got to tell people something **revolutionary.** It's got to be something wild, something that gets their attention. You have to make them a strong promise. Get them pumped up, and they'll get interested. Make them a strong promise, or tell them about something outrageous you're about to

---

reveal, and then go on to something else for a moment. **Here's a working headline, an example of this first step:** "I'm going to show you how to make $4,854 a day while sitting in your underwear! And I promise, you'll never have to put in more than 30 minutes a day. But first…" **Then you go on to something else. But now they're hooked!** This keeps them reading. It snaps them into attention. There's nothing new in this first step. In fact, in the late 1700s a man named Dr. Johnson said, **"The big promise is the soul of an advertisement."** That was known 300 years ago. In Step #1, you're making people a big promise. It's bold! It's outrageous! It gets them excited and wakes them up!

Listen: More than ever before, people *need* something like that. **To wake people up it's got to be huge in order, because people these days feel like that they've heard and seen everything.** They feel jaded. The things that used to excite them don't anymore. They're skeptical. They doubt everything. They're immune to hype; they don't trust anything.

So your message has to cut through the clutter. **It has to be unique enough that it doesn't even *sound* like hype.** For instance, consider an opportunity that lets people save 30-70% off their grocery purchases on over 10,000 different items—with free delivery. It's all done over the Internet. They can scroll through over 10,000 discounted grocery items and pick what they want, pay, and Federal Express will bring a box to their door. Now, that's big! It's bold! It's outrageous! People will look at it and say, "What? Could this really be true?" It wakes people up, and that's what you have to do! **Your promise has to be big enough, bold enough, and unique enough that it just cuts through all the clutter out there, snaps people up, and gets their attention.**

This stratagem gets people into your letter, especially if you're writing a long-form sales letter where you want them to take a considerable amount of time to read your offer. **You make a big promise to them; you do something to get them to stop and pay attention.** This works on the Internet or by mail, but I'm thinking specifically about how, if you mail a sales letter to someone, they're probably opening their mail over their trashcan or close to their recycling bin or their shredder. You only have a few seconds to make an impression and get them to decide that your offer is worth paying any attention to. As they're flipping through their mail they see their water bill... and they put that aside. They know they've got to pay that. They see an ad for Wal-Mart and, well, they really don't want to stop and pay attention to that, so that goes in the recycling bin. Then they get to your offer. The envelope looks promising, so they open it up and see a big headline, a big guarantee. And, of course, because you've done a good job of making sure that person is a good prospect for your offer, they see that outrageous headline on your sales letter and they stop. Maybe they were just planning on pitching it in the trash, **but they see your offer—your big, bold claim—and it stops them in their tracks.** They're looking for the big bold benefit you just promised them... and then you skip over it.

You don't reveal it right away; you jump right to something else. Pretty soon they've read to the bottom of the first page, still looking for information on that big bold promise you made them—so they turn to page 2. Soon they're on page 3, and they're into the letter, and maybe you *never* reveal the main reason or the main benefit or promise that you told them about on page 1. They have to buy your product to get that, or go to your website, or take whatever action you're trying to get them to take. **But by making that big, bold, outrageous claim or**

guarantee or promise in the headline, you got them to pay attention and at least take a look at your offer. Not all of them will respond, of course, but you want them to at least take a look.

That's the purpose of Step 1. You tell them something amazing, something beyond belief, something revolutionary — something that's going to make them pay attention. **A headline that doesn't do any of those things is easily dismissed.** If someone's opening their mail over a trashcan, they're probably going to discard any message that doesn't jump out at them or make them pay attention. There's a huge difference between a bland, boring headline one that attracts people and one that makes them stop and pay attention.

For example: If you have a product for the diet industry, i.e. for people who are looking for a miracle weight-loss plan, you want your headline to make some outrageous statement about how much weight they can lose and how easy it's going to be. Of course, you have to be strictly truthful here; you can't just make your statement up. **It has to be a factual, legitimate headline.** It can't be just something you make up to get people to stop and pay attention, or else they'll come to find out that your offer is insincere. But still, you want the headline that you're making to make

> The <u>more</u> money a customer spends — the <u>less</u> problems they cause you. There are exceptions to this, but they are few and far between.

some kind of a crazy, almost unbelievable, claim so that they have to read to figure out what the heck you're talking about! **You've got to get them beyond page 1 and into your offer.**

It's the same way when you're marketing online. People are searching for whatever your offer is, and the headline they see when they visit your website has to get them to stop and pay attention, to keep reading instead of going elsewhere. **One of the big problems marketers experience online is the fact that people are looking for instant info.** If they get to your website, that's the very first, minimal step; it's almost like a pre-Step 1, really. Once they're there, you have to get them to stay rather than click onto something else. On the Internet it's so easy for someone to move on. **If your site doesn't look appealing, they head back to the search engine directory and find another link to click.**

So right away, they've got to see some kind of outrageous guarantee or promise or benefit in big bold typeface. Tell them something revolutionary; give them something wild! Make an outrageous claim — something to get them excited and make them interested. If you can't get their interest right away, they're going to move on to something else because they're busy, they're bored, or they're skeptical. They've got other things going on, so it's easy to say no. **That's why you've got to give them some kind of an outrageous statement, just to keep their interest and make them want to keep reading.**

Again, most people are jaded. We doubt things, because we've seen all kinds of promises, many of them false. **So when something comes along that gets *you* excited, that should be kind of an acid test!** And this thing I told you about as an example earlier, which gives people the opportunity to sell a membership that lets other people save 30-70% off their grocery bill — I got excited about that one myself! I got so pumped up that I almost called up a couple of my key staff members on Sunday, which is something I *never* do. If something excites you like that and you're somewhat jaded or doubtful, then that's a pretty good test (as long as you're similar to your customers, as you should be).

STEP 2: You tell your prospects that what you have for them is a variation of something that's already making tons of money. This gives them something familiar to link to. It's a positioning concept. You're talking about something they already know about, and it makes it easier to understand and relate to the new thing you're trying to present. Now you're speaking their language.

The first time I remember ever using this six-step formula includes my best example of Step 2. This was back in 1993. Computer bulletin boards, which were the precursor of the Internet, were the hot thing. There were people who were advertising on up to 60,000 or more of these bulletin boards— absolutely free! This was a few years before the Worldwide Web came along and rushed the computer bulletin board industry.

We were among the very first people who started working with Bulletin Board Service (BBS) experts, like Alan R. Bechtold, to show our clients how they could advertise for free on thousands of boards. In trying to show them just how amazing and how revolutionary this really was, we gave them examples of traditional advertising; that was Step 2. We showed them what it cost for them to set up and run a classified ad in dozens of the national magazines they were already familiar with. And then, only then, were they ready to wake up to this valuable new solution. **Our strategy gave them something to link to, and gave what we were selling much more perceived value.**

What you want to do here is make a leap from the familiar to the unfamiliar. This is especially important if you're jumping into a new thing that there's little or no understanding of. Usually you want to avoid those things, because they're unlikely to be successful; as they say, the pioneers are the ones who get scalped. We've had friends who ventured into uncharted waters, basically inventing new things that really hadn't been heard of before. It's like swimming upstream, because you have to educate people on why they should even bother with the new product or service.

You probably remember the Segway, which debuted about ten years ago. **It was by no means the revolutionary new product that its manufacturers built it up to be, but the buzz really caught people's attention.** They had a code name for it, and had all these patents they'd been granted, and they were launching this brand new product that was going to revolutionize the world! They built it up so big, and then when they launched it they said, "Here it is… the Segway!" And what is it? A little two-wheeled scooter thing you stand on, and it's got a gyro sensor; by moving your body around you make the thing go forwards, backwards, turn sideways, or whatever. It goes a whopping 12 miles an hour. Well, it was pretty much a failure. Some police departments bought a bunch of them, and some malls bought them and used them for security guards and things like that; but generally, the general public had no use for them, despite the hype. **They tried to create something brand new that people didn't even really have any concept of or need for, and it flopped.**

> **Great entrepreneurs love change.** We embrace it! We need it. We crave it. The rest of the world is our exact opposite in this regard.

Step 2 is crucial when you've got something completely new. I don't know how they could have applied it with the Segway; but still, when you're trying to get someone to understand something they don't understand, **the best way to do that is to move them from something they "get" first and then build a bridge to the thing that they *don't* get, which is what you're trying to educate them on.** When something's brand new, you *must* start with the familiar if you have any hope of making money.

One of the things we're working on right now is educating local retail businesses on how to use affiliate programs. People understand online affiliate programs well enough; they've been around for a while. Well, knowing that, why aren't local retail businesses using affiliate programs to do things *offline* to help local people make money, or to provide better gifts, premiums, or discounts? So we're developing a program to help them do so. **This program uses the Step 2 strategy: We take something familiar — an Internet affiliate program — and move them from their understanding of that into how you could make affiliate programs work offline.** They already understand online affiliate programs, and this is just taking that offline. Again, you start with something they understand, and move it into the area that they don't. It helps them build a picture in their mind of what you're trying to do for them, or the benefit they're going to receive when they buy your product or buy your service. **Start with what they know and build upon it.**

Maybe you've built a better mousetrap. What you do is take the basic mousetrap design and say, "Here, you understand how this works. Well, I've built a better one; here's what it does, and here's why it's bigger and better, faster and cheaper." **Instead of going straight for what they don't know and having to educate them on that, you build parallels between something that's familiar to them.** By doing that, you're a lot closer to the sale.

Remember, Step 1 is: It's got to be bold! It's got to be new! It's got to be revolutionary! **The problem with that is that if it's *too* new, people won't understand it.** Think about the Segway. People really didn't know what it was. They didn't understand it, so they were skeptical of it. Most still are. **People want new things, but they have to be linked with what they already know about.** If it's too new, they're going to freak out. They're going to go from being excited to being scared and nervous very quickly.

STEP 3: Go into all the problems with the original variation that you talked about in Step #2. In other words, talk about the bad stuff. Before you can reveal the good points, **give them an example of something that's already working, something they're already familiar with, and then enumerate the negatives.**

Going back to the computer bulletin boards, we were showing people how they could advertise on thousands of these bulletin boards, absolutely free. People got so excited about that. The promise was big; it was bold; it was audacious! Then we showed them in Step #2 that the program was connected with something they knew, but was better. We told them that if they wanted to run a classified ad with traditional space advertising, here's how much it would cost, and here's what they would have to go through. That's where Step 3 steps in. One of the advantages of BBS was that you could deliver information products without any hard physical costs. **There were all these money saving and labor saving advantages over the traditional way—but you couldn't appreciate those advantages until you got to see a clear example of how it was before.** So before you even explain what your new breakthrough is, start going through all of the problems, the headaches, the hassles, the high cost of what it would take to do something that they're already familiar with. Only then can you go on to the next steps.

When you introduce a product into the marketplace, one of the first things people want to know is, "Why do I need this? Why is this different than what's out there? Why is this better than what I already can get? What makes this worth me spending money on? What in the marketplace does this compare to?" **People are instantly going to make comparisons in their heads, and in most cases, they have the ability to find things to compare it to.** Even if your product is unique, there's probably something similar they could do with their money that might, in their minds, be a viable alternative. **You need to answer their concerns by playing up the differences between what used to be and what now is, with the way your product solves the problems and challenges that plague the original, the thing that they already understand. Then you talk about the solution you've created, and the benefits that result.**

> There are only two things that will make you money in any business: marketing and innovation. Everything else is a business expense. — *Peter Drucker*

Here's another quick example. We have a product where we take something that's existed for many years in the affiliate industry—the standard method of paying affiliate commissions—and rework it. Normally, when you're a website affiliate and you bring them a customer, they pay you if and only if that customer makes a purchase. Now, three things could happen here. One is that the person goes to the website, doesn't buy anything today, and you don't get anything for sending them there. Option 2 is that they make a purchase today, you get paid a commission for referring them, and they never return to the site. Option 3 is that the person becomes a lifelong customer of that website, buys lots of stuff on an ongoing basis, and you get *nothing* besides the original commission they paid you for the initial referral. **Our version essentially pays lifetime commissions. We feel you should be paid commission no matter how long a person does business with us.**

We've created a new model here. **We've taken what's already very well known in the Internet marketing world and kicked it up a notch.** We tell people that we think there's a better way to pay affiliates; not only are you going to get paid a commission if the person buys something today, but even if they choose not to buy today, if they wait and then buy something six months from now, **you *still* brought them to us, so we're going to reward you.** Beyond that, even if they do buy something today, we're going to reward you for bringing them to us by paying you a commission every time that customer does any business with us. As long as we maintain a relationship with that client, we're going to continue paying you an affiliate commission, because you introduced them to us.

I think that's a good example of Step 3. **We take something well-understood, talk about the problems inherent with that model, and then show how we've improved on it.** By being a part of this new kind of affiliate program, you can set yourself up to get paid not only today but any time that person does business with us in the future. That's another example of how you can use Step 3 to build on Step 2.

STEP #4: Show them that your new discovery eliminates all or most of the problems that you gave them from your example of something they're already familiar with. This step gives them more of the good stuff, less of the bad stuff. It increases their desire and makes them want it even more. **Now, all of a sudden, they're hooked.** If you did it right, this leads to the next step, which I'll talk about momentarily.

First, let's go back to our affiliate program: the Guaranteed Money Discovery, as we're calling it. With Step #2, we talk about affiliate programs in general; we make people comfortable with the fact that they already know a lot about them. In Step #3, we provide examples of the problems that afflict affiliate programs. **Then, in Step #4, we start revealing our solution: an affiliate program that keeps on paying you for as long as people buy from us, for the life of our company.** Every time a sale is made, our affiliates get paid. Only when people understand how it works in a traditional way (Step #2), and then when they understand all of the problems that are associated with the traditional way (Step #3), are they fully ready for Step 4: the solution! You can only truly value or appreciate something, or even understand it properly, when you have something to compare it with. That's not just a marketing principle, it's a principle of life and business. **The more you have to compare it with, the more you're going to understand it. So that's when we provide them with our solution.**

People are always making comparisons. But when you get right down to it, our job as copywriters/marketers is to make those comparisons for them, since they're going to whether you do it or not. **You want to compare what you're selling against something that makes your deal look even better.** You never compare apples to apples; you compare apples to oranges. You always try to position your solution. You make whatever you sell much more appealing by what you choose to compare it with.

This is industry specific. You're talking about selling to your target marketplace, so you know what their problems are, and you've written your sales copy so you're pointing out their pain, the challenges and struggles they're experiencing on a daily basis; and then you give them examples of things they understand. Then you talk about all the problems, and hit 'em with your solution. **By this point, if you've done your job in the selling process, the pain they're experiencing is real.** You're not *causing* them pain; you're just pointing it out to them. **You've reminded them of the struggle they're already having.**

Consider the weight loss industry. If someone's struggling to lose weight, **they're looking for a solution — not necessarily a particular product.** They're in pain, and want something that works for them. **If you're selling to the business opportunity market, you're probably selling to people who are looking for a solution to the pain caused by money woes.** They want to make more money, they want to have more financial independence, and they're struggling with that. Maybe they're up to their eyeballs in debt, and so there's serious pain there.

> If you don't know it can't be done, you can do it.

All throughout the first three steps of this formula the pain has been building up. **Because Step 4 demonstrates how your discovery eliminates all their problems, this increases their desire.** It makes them want your product and, at this point, they're feeling a little relief, because they know there's a solution on the horizon. All they have to do is follow the advice you're getting ready to give them. There's no way they're going to stop reading, because they want the benefit you promised them under Step 1. **They want the relief from the pain.** Now, it may take you a while to get to that point, because you've got to cover a lot of examples in the previous steps. **You want to make it agonizingly real for them.** Many of our sales letters are 24, 36, even 48 pages long. People often say, "My goodness! Is anybody going to read 24 to 36 pages?" and the answer is: "If they're qualified prospects, sure they are." And even those who don't read the entire letter will skim it. **In fact, we write the letters to be skimmed, not necessarily read.** The point is, it takes time to build your case. The examples just help to make it real, so people can internalize it and personalize it.

STEP #5: <u>Show</u> <u>your</u> <u>prospect</u> <u>a</u> <u>brief</u> "<u>sizzle</u>" <u>example</u> <u>of</u> <u>what</u> <u>your</u> <u>new</u> <u>discovery</u> <u>can</u> <u>do</u> <u>for</u> <u>them</u>. Give them a glimpse of the greatest benefit. **That ties in with the headline you gave them in the beginning.** Take this BBS example I've been using. In Step #5, we provided a sample of how they could advertise free on computer bulletin boards, and kept pointing back to the examples we'd already used—things they understood, and how much those older strategies would cost them in time, money, and effort. We sold millions and millions of dollars worth of product, and then took a variation of that sales letter to sell websites, too. **We probably rewrote that sales letter for 10 years and reused it in various forms.**

And keep in mind: You do have to go through these steps in the proper sequence. If you were just to go from Step 1 to Step 5, you wouldn't make nearly as many sales. You have to make sure you have the intervening steps in place. **That's what we call the "build up," and it's absolutely crucial.** You've got to introduce the problem, and make the pain real—so that Steps 4 and 5 really hit home. If you tried to skip Steps 2 and 3, you'd be shooting yourself in the foot. **You can't skip around; the process is a progression from one to the other, in order.**

It helps them develop an affinity with you; otherwise, there's no reason why they would even give you the time of day, much less stop and open your envelope. **By the time you get to Step 5, though, they're feeling good about you. Every other step along the way is intended to move the customer from cold prospect status to someone who's willing to respond to your offer:** from a point where they don't know you, don't trust you, have no reason why they would want to stop and give you anything... to a point where they actually *want* what you're offering enough to take a chance on someone they don't really know anything about. You need to get the point where they're willing to put their credit card number down on the form and drop it in the mail, or fax it, or go online and give you their order.

By now, they've seen themselves using your product, and you want to show them what their life will look like with the benefits they'll receive. If you're selling a business opportunity, the flash and sizzle could be their new lifestyle after they've received the benefits... *after* they've purchased your product. If it's in the health industry, you're showing them what life will be like when they're receiving the benefits or have the result you promised them in your headline. If they're a single male, they may imagine themselves with six-pack abs and toned muscles on the beach, with women admiring them. If it's the ladies you're targeting, they could envision themselves being stared at by guys as they're wearing their bikini and lying out in the sun. **The benefit is no longer an abstract idea; now they're living it in their mind.** But this is just a brief thing: You want to leave them hanging on that thought, and then move on to the next step. But this step is important, because it makes them visualize themselves receiving those benefits you promised them. I hope you can see how all of this does flow together. It really is a logical process, one that makes a lot of common sense. And once you're aware of it, you'll see how other people are using variations on a theme here.

> The _why_ to do something always comes before the _how_ to do it! *This is the secret behind all great achievers.*

STEP #6 is the money step, otherwise known as the close. This is where you tell them how hard it would be for them to figure all this out on their own—how much time, work, and money that it took for you to do so. Then you show them how they can get everything put together for them, ready to go, just by sending you their money. If you set it up right, it makes the close very natural; each steps leads inexorably to the next. **You brought up the problem, you agitated it, you made it real, you offered a solution, and now they want what you have.** If they were to do it on their own, it would be very difficult. **So they're ready to give you their money, because you've put it all together for them.**

With the BBS example, we made a bold promise, built it up by showing how difficult ordinary advertising was and how simple BBS advertising was, made them feel the pain, and showed them the solution. All of a sudden, they just gave us their money! Within six months, we brought in over 2.5 million in sales. **The close ought to be like that: a very natural thing.** If you've set it up right and built it up properly, when it comes time for the close people see so much value, so much advantage… and they see that the promise you made them in Step #1 was absolutely true. **They go from being skeptical and jaded to being so excited they're ready to give you their money... and that's Step #6.**

Many people think selling is basically twisting people's arms, that you almost have to con people out of their money. **No, you've got to do something to get them to give up their money willingly.** Selling has a bad rap because of coercive tactics; so some people shy away from the close, which is a big mistake. It's important to remember that if you've targeted the right person—someone who's looking for the kind of benefits your product or service delivers—then you'd be doing them a disservice not to offer your solution to them. So the close should be a natural part of the process; it should be a logical next step. **The rest of the process is pointless if you don't go for the close.**

You've made the big, bold, outrageous statement. You've made them stop and pay attention to your offer. You've shown them why they're in pain. You've pointed out the problems and challenges they're facing, and ultimately you reveal why your product or service solves that pain they're having. **When you do those things in order, that person is going to be ready to buy.** Now, that doesn't mean that everybody *will* buy; in fact, most of the time, most people don't. As I've mentioned, in Direct Response you can make good money even with bad numbers. In some cases, as many as 95 out of 100 can say "no" and you still can make good money in DRM. **So don't get too hung up on how many people say "no" versus how many people say "yes."**

The point I'm trying to make is that if you do follow this process properly, assuming you've targeted the right kind of prospect, at the very least they're going to say, "I see myself using this product. I see myself getting the benefit." Some will buy, because this process is a progression that leads naturally to the sale, as long as you've chosen the right kinds of buyers. **When they get to the point where you make them an irresistible offer, it's going to be difficult for them to say no,**

because they've already visualized themselves receiving the benefits your product or service delivers. Once they get to that place where they see themselves having lost the weight, or they see themselves as a millionaire, they don't want to go back. They don't want to be in pain anymore. **Your product is offering them the ultimate opportunity to alleviate that pain.** It's saying, "All you have to do now is buy my magic solution in a bottle," or whatever the case may be. You're offering them a final solution to their pain.

If you've done everything right you'll get the biggest percentage of your prospects to say "yes" to your offer. At least give it a try! This is a very simple formula. It's something you can easily learn the basics of, but that you can take a lifetime to master. **You'll eventually find success by using this formula and keeping these six points in mind.** It's a great formula, and I'm glad that I was able to share it with you.

And by the way, I'd love to see your sales letters! If you're using this formula for writing your own sales copy, send it in to us and let us take a look at it. **We'll offer tips and strategies on how to make it better.** This formula really can make you millions of dollars—and I'm dead serious about that. I can't guarantee that you will, but I know that you *can*, because these are the same things that we and a lot of other people are doing.

So go out there and do it!

11

Concepts First and Details Last!

This secret I have to share with you is very simple, like everything else I've shared so far — and yet it's very profound at the same time. I call it "Concepts First and Details Last." You've got to think it bigger, and yet you have to see things as simpler than ever before. **You must develop a strong personal philosophy that keeps you moving forward at full speed, no matter what the obstacles are.** This philosophy, which is made up of your core beliefs, will help you achieve bigger results in less time. **Too many people get bogged down in the details.** Concepts First, Details Last; don't even worry about how you're going to do things. **Instead, spend your time thinking about the "why" to the thing;** spend your time working on your goals and developing all the reasons why you want to make millions of dollars.

Much of what I've covered here is conceptual in nature. **You still have to figure out a way to do all these things, but the more you focus on the details, the more you're going to get bogged down** — the more you're going to become overwhelmed, frustrated, and confused. **If you keep going back to the reasons why all these things work, or the general nature of the basics, you're going to be fully empowered.** You develop your belief system, the things that help to guide you; and one of the things that I hope you've gained from all of this is an understanding that none of this is easy. There are people out there who want to totally mislead you when it comes to getting rich; they want to tell you that it's a snap. But they're liars — and surely there's a part of you that knows that you can't just make money that easily. There's a price to pay for it. Now, the point is that once you fall in love with the ideas I've shared with you, and once you become passionate about marketing, once you become passionate about product-development work and all the things you do to attract and retain customers, *then* **it becomes fun or challenging. It becomes interesting and exciting; it becomes a way of life,** so you're willing to do more than the average person. And when you are, that's when you're going to develop the skills necessary to make millions and millions of dollars.

That's when it becomes more like a lifestyle or a hobby. Some of the things that are very difficult for you to learn will give you a tremendous sense of pride and satisfaction, once you learn them, like you can't even imagine right now — a feeling of confidence and power because you've mastered these things. **People tend to place the largest value on the things we pay the biggest price to gain, and some of these skills can make you millions of dollars, just as they have for me.** If everybody had these skills, then everybody would be making millions of dollars, wouldn't they? And if everybody was rich, why would *you* want to be rich? Part of the attraction of getting rich is the fact that it's the trophy, the prize, the catch, the goal that we set out for; it's the way we keep score, the way that we rise above it all. It's not just egotism. You can always look at your net worth and know how well you're doing, but what I've have done is kept journals over the years. I've thought through my own personal philosophy, my own concepts and my own beliefs — and I want to share with you some of the core ideas that have helped me achieve my success. **I've got 39 powerful, core ideas that have served me and have helped me to be, do and have more of what I really want.** I'd like for you think about these 39 ideas, and maybe some of them can be part of your core philosophy as well. **These are part of my belief system and part of my guidance, the things that help keep me moving forward.**

NUMBER 1: Go as far as you can see, and when you get there, you'll be able to see even farther. So many people are confused because they're trying to figure it all out too fast; they want all the answers *now*. **They want to try to figure it all out before they get started.** Forget that: go as far as you possibly can, take it as far as you can take it, and when you get there you'll be in a better place. You'll be more knowledgeable, you'll know more, and you'll be able to see even

> **W**hat are you willing to do? The answer to these six words will determine how much money you will ultimately make.

farther. So don't think that you have to have it all figured out; you don't. You'll figure it out as you go.

NUMBER 2: "He who flies the highest can see the farthest." That's what conceptual thinking is all about. When you're detail-oriented, you tend to see everything from the bottom up; you get bogged down in the minutia. **When you think conceptually, you're thinking from the top down; you're able to see it bigger and think it simpler.** So set your goals very high, and see the simplicity in everything we've shared here. Making millions of dollars doesn't have to be that complicated when you stay focused on the basics, when you don't worry about how you're going to do everything. **When you set your goals high and keep it simple, that's the one thing that's going to separate you from all the other people who are working with you.** You're going to be able to see things from the top down and know just how simple all this is. So fly high, and always answer that question, "How high is high?" What are you really capable of doing; how far can you go? Set those high goals; don't be afraid to do that, and you'll see even further than most people.

NUMBER 3: You must develop the heart of the lion and the mind of the fox. For years now I've had a little fox and a little lion, and I keep them where I can see them at all times. **I've thought a lot about that: the heart of the lion, the mind of the fox.** The fox is a cunning animal, and you've got to be a bit like that in business; you're always on the edge, you're always aware, you're always looking around, **you're always watching people's actions instead of just listening to what they say.** You realize that people are self-centered by nature; the more you have, the more people want to get it. So you've got to be on guard; you really do. You've got to be careful too. And then you've got to have the heart of the lion: the lion is bold and audacious, the king of the jungle — and it does take a little bit of audacity.

One of my greatest stories is the story of Solo Flex. The guy who founded that company was a jet pilot who flew high rollers back and forth to Las Vegas, mostly to and from L.A. or San Francisco. Over a period of time, he got to know some of the regulars. They'd get up to the cruising altitude, he'd flip it over to automatic pilot, and he would go spend forty-five minutes or an hour talking with these people. They got to know each other well. So here he is, at age fifty or so, and he's making pretty good money; he has a six-figure income coming in, he's a chartered jet pilot, and one morning he just seized on this powerful question: "What makes these people any different than I am?" **The answer to the question was: audacity.** These people were just audacious; they were bold. That's it. They were no smarter than he was, they were no better looking than he was, they had no more special abilities or talents; it was just audacity. They each had the heart of the lion, and that's what some of this really does take. **You've got to suspend all of your fear and go for it.** Don't be afraid to fall, and just keep getting up every time you *do* fall.

NUMBER 4: In every business deal, always assume there's something, or a series of somethings, that the other party is holding back from you. You have to be careful — that's sort of like the mind of the fox. Always be careful; always. **I've tried to hold nothing back from you in this book, but I promise you, in every deal you have to assume that there's something that they're not telling you.** Just assume it, even if it's not true. It'll help you stand guard; it'll help you be very careful. Here's an example: once upon a time, Eileen and I needed the help of an attorney. I'll never forget this: he was asking us to sign this contract that would have made him many, many thousands of dollars, and he was trying to scare us a little. We were in trouble; we needed some fast answers, and he was, I remember, using high-pressure tactics on us. Eileen and I were in his office, and I recall watching him very carefully — and I saw a little bead of sweat start rolling down his face as he was waiting for us to sign this contract. I got up and left his office, and Eileen followed me; and we didn't sign the contract. Pretty soon, we drove off and we found another lawyer who turned out to be a great person who worked with us for a number of years. **The other guy was trying to use a number of tactics on us, trying to manipulate us, trying to scare us.** Look, you've always got to watch people, watch them carefully. Always think that they're holding something back from you; then you'll be on guard.

NUMBER 5: You've got to work on yourself as hard you work on your business. These ideas in this book are simple, really. You'll see that there's nothing all that complicated about what I'm sharing, and yes, a lot of it's redundant. That's because a lot of these ideas are really simple by nature. **It's all about working through the fears and the insecurities, and all the false and limited beliefs that have held you back.** That's going to be the challenge; that's going to be the determinator of how you use these secrets, whether you go full force and use them to make millions of dollars, or whether you hold back. **It's about dealing with yourself and it's setting higher goals; it's about working through your fears and insecurities; it's about deciding that you're going to go for it, even if you don't have it all figured out.** So work on yourself; write down a list of all of the things you're afraid of, all the things that have held you back up to now, and be completely honest with yourself. There are plenty of good books out there that can help. One of the best books I can recommend was written in the late 1980s by Susan Jeffers; it's called *Feel the Fear and Do It Anyway*. I would encourage you to get that book. **You've got to work on yourself constantly.** If you're not making the kind of money you want to be making, then there's something that's

> Before you can inspire with emotion, you must be swamped with it yourself. — *Winston Churchill*

stopping you; and until and unless you work on yourself, you're never going to figure it out.

NUMBER 6: Work *on* your business, and not *in* it.
You've got to be the architect of your business; you have to be the general of the war. You can't be on the front lines. **I would advise you to find other people to manage your business, so you can focus all your time on all the things that are necessary to** attract and retain customers. Work on it, look at your business in a conceptual way, and you see the simplicity of it.

NUMBER 7: See everything from the top down, and not the bottom up; that's what concepts are all about. They let you see how simple everything is — and it really *is* simple. I've tried to share that with you throughout this entire book.

NUMBER 8: Self-discipline leads to self-confidence.
You've got to force yourself to do the things that are necessary, that will make you the most money. **You have to force yourself to learn these new skills of being able to write copy, develop product, do things that make you a great marketer.** A lot of times it doesn't feel good, and even when you get good at it, you still have to force yourself to do it. You'll have moments when you're on fire, when you're so excited, when it's not work at all. You'll have moments when it's fun, it's interesting, it's challenging, and the energy is there and you just want to do it all, and it's easy. Then you have other days when it's very, very difficult.

Remember: the professional does it when they don't feel like doing it. You don't just do it when you feel like doing it, you do it all the time. **You discipline yourself, *force* yourself to work.** I got up at 5:00 this morning and wrote copy until my hands hurt, finishing up a sales letter. Some days, it just comes flowing out of me; today it didn't. Today I had to work at it. I've been doing this for twenty years now and it's still work, although sometimes it's a great pleasure. So, you've got to take the good and the bad, and the more you do to force yourself to do the things that you know are in your best interest, the better you're going to feel about yourself — and that does lead to self-confidence.

NUMBER 9: This Jim Rohn quote became my mantra, and I want it to be yours: **"Don't wish things were easier; wish that you were better."** So many people want things to be easy. When life gets tough, they fantasize about an easy life. Jim says, "Look: just wish you were better, because if you were, you wouldn't be faced with such obstacles." That's one of the cool things about growing and developing, and it's one of the ways I can see true growth in myself. I meet entrepreneurs who are on the path I've been on for 20 years, and I see them struggling with things I used to struggle with. I see them going through problems I used to live with — but they're not problems for me anymore. I see them getting upset about things that used to destroy me; but those things don't bother me now, and I know it's because I've gotten better. **I've practiced what I've preached, I've put in the hours, I've done the work, I've developed the skills. You've got to do it too.** Wish that you were better, because if you *were* better, you wouldn't have such problems. You'd be able to solve some of the things you can't solve right now.

NUMBER 10: It's always better to have a valuable resource and not need it, than to need it and not have it. That's true with so many things. A valuable resource can be great people in your life, or it can be money in the bank; it could be products that you've got waiting in the wings, all kinds of promotions that you can rework. It can be certain things that you've learned. It's always better to have that resource and not need it, than to be in a position where you need something and don't have it. **Just think about what that can mean for you, and think about what a resource is: something that offers you value.**

> The marketers' most important asset is his or her knack for putting themselves in the position of their customers and for addressing their most important needs.

NUMBER 11: All that glitters is not gold. That's one of my most important concepts. There are all kinds of distractions out there, all kinds of things you can get into, and there's lots of different kinds of glitter; but **you've got to think about what's most important all the time, and realize that some of that glitter is just fool's gold.**

NUMBER 12: A quote from Robert DeRopp, a great philosopher: **"Seek above all else a game that's worth playing, and then play it as if your entire life and sanity depended on it, for it does."** I think the greatest game on Earth is the game of business: the money acquisition game, learning all the things I've talked about that have to do with developing product, attracting customers, separating yourself from every other competitor in your marketplace, continuing to do business over and over with the same clients, who continue to give you more and more money for larger profits every time. **This is a great game, so play it like one!**

NUMBER 13: One day at a time; let go, and let God; this too shall pass. Yeah, I've had to learn that. It's easy to get overwhelmed; **but all you've got to do is just worry about today, and let tomorrow take care of itself.** If you're putting everything you can into today, you're fine. Think of it as a brick wall, a solid brick wall that's your whole life, and each day is one of those bricks, and think about what you're doing with it. Most people are just heaping those bricks outside; **their lives are directionless.** They're going nowhere, they're achieving nothing, they're not doing anything big with their lives. They're taking that brick everyday and just throwing it onto some great big pile. I want you to think about this: **Don't worry about the future, take care of today, let the future take care of itself, and don't get overwhelmed.** There were things, back in the early-1990s, that used to cause me to almost have a heart attack. Here I was, in my late 20s, early 30s, and my chest was hurting and I'd get so angry — but now those things don't even bother me. I've learned to let it go, and you've got to, too. That's one of the things I see in all these up-and-comers who are on the same path: I see them getting so bothered about things that used to bother me, and there's no need for that. **Just let it go.**

NUMBER 14: You must be willing to lose a few (or many) battles so you can win the war. You have to decide what war is to you, but be willing to lose a few battles; be quietly effective. Don't worry about fighting every battle; you're going to wear yourself out. Just be willing to stay focused on your goals. Nothing else means anything.

NUMBER 15: The "why" to do something is always more important than the "how." That's where concepts and goals come in: knowing why you want to make millions of dollars. I *know* you want to make millions; only a fool would invest in this book if they didn't. You've got to ask yourself why. **You'll figure out the "how to do it" if the "why to do it" is big enough.**

NUMBER 16: "Selling is serving" — that's a Ray Kroc

quote. Well, a lot of people don't want to be salespeople. Salespeople have a bad rep. A salesperson is somebody who's offering something that's worth so much value that the money they're asking for in exchange should pale by comparison. **Their whole focus is on serving, whatever serving means to your marketplace; focus on that.** That's what selling really is.

NUMBER 17: A successful life is a series of successful days. Take care of today and tomorrow will take care of itself. Everybody's worried about the future; well, you don't have to be, as long as you're taking care of every single day, right here and now.

NUMBER 18: You've got to be willing to do what nobody else wants to do. You see, a lot of this is difficult, in the beginning especially, and that's not popular. If you want to go out there and buy some, well, there are magic programs where people are trying to tell you how simple and easy it is. And it *is* simple; that's part of what this last principle I'm sharing with you is all about. **You've got to *keep* it simple. But you also have to be very disciplined; you have to be willing to put in the time, put in the work, put in the effort, and you've got to be willing to do the things most people aren't going to do.**

NUMBER 19: Keep your eyes on the stars, and always let your reach exceed your grasp. You've always got to be pushing for more to answer the questions, "How high is high?" and "What are you really capable of?" Set your goals high; keep dreaming big dreams. **When you keep your eyes on the stars, you're willing to endure the problems and challenges that stop some people.** There are going to be speed bumps on your road, so keep dreaming those big dreams. Don't be afraid to do that.

Number 20: Don't drive down the road with one foot on the gas pedal and the other on the brake. Too many people are trying to be so cautious all the time that they're afraid to drive. Look, race car drivers will tell you that the secret is to just stay totally focused on the road ahead. That's it; that's all you've got to do. **Keep your eyes right on the road, and just go for it. Just drive; don't hold back.**

NUMBER 21: The things you tell yourself about yourself are the most important things. You're better and stronger than you think you are. Keep telling yourself good things about yourself. **Don't listen to your inner critic; don't listen to the exterior critics in your life.** Write down all the things you're the best at, that you're strong in; and that goes back to what we talked about in Number 5. Work on yourself as hard as you work on your business. Be your own best friend. **Life is too short to go through it by second-guessing yourself, criticizing yourself and tearing yourself down.**

> Never promote a product or service that you can't explain in 3 minutes! Or at least cover the major benefits!

NUMBER 22: Business is a combination of art, science, sport, politics, and war. Think about those concepts. **It's creative, it's artistic; it's also scientific.** There are principles at work here. These are the same principles that have made us millions of dollars. It's also a sport, and there are ways of keeping score. It's somewhat political; sometimes you can't always be direct with people. It's like war too; it's a battle. Try to keep that in your mind all the time. It's not just about making money. You noticed I didn't use the word "money" in there at all. It's art, science, sports, politics, and war; those are the concepts to keep you moving forward.

NUMBER 23: Marketing is like chess. The masters of marketing are always thinking three steps ahead at all times. Remember, chess is pretty simple; there are only six basic pieces, and a few basic moves for you to learn. Once you have those moves down, that's it. Marketing is like that too.

NUMBER 24: Making money is the greatest game on Earth. Play it, and keep playing it. **It's not just something you do for the money, it's something you do for joy and satisfaction; it'll fill your life up.** You'll keep wanting to go for bigger and better things; you'll keep trying to improve yourself and your game. You won't just make money so you can sit on your butt and do nothing. There will be no such thing as retirement to you. **There may be semi-retirement, but your business will be about things that you truly enjoy.** It's your passion; it's your skill set. It's the greatest game on Earth; play it, have some fun. Remember what DeRopp said: "Seek above all else a game worth playing and then play it as if your entire life and sanity depended up on it, for it truly does."

NUMBER 25: "Fear destroys more people than any other one thing." The brilliant Ralph Waldo Emerson said that. If you really knew you could handle anything and everything that happens to you, what would there be to fear? Absolutely nothing. **We're only afraid because there's something inside us that doesn't believe we can handle it. Well, I'm telling you — you** *can* **handle it.** You handle it one day at a time, one brick at a time. You handle it by continuing to go as far as you can see; and then when you get there, you'll see further. You don't need to take it all in at once. **Remember that fear is the enemy; you've got to conquer it.**

NUMBER 26: This is the thing I say to myself a lot of

mornings — like today, when I didn't want to get out of bed. It's a Shakespeare quote: **"To thine own self be true."** You've got to be true to yourself, true to your goals, what you're trying to accomplish in life. **Keep moving forward, in spite of whether you want to or not; just keep doing it.**

NUMBER 27: In everything that you do, think it bigger and see it simpler. That's what Concepts First and Details Last is all about. Everybody else is getting bogged down in details; everybody else is focused on all of the little complexities involved in every major project. You can't do it. You've got to think bigger and see it simpler.

NUMBER 28: "You can have everything in life you want, if you'll only help enough people get what *they* want." This is a Zig Ziglar quote. **And notice I said "want," not "need."** There's a big difference here. You're helping people get what they want. Well, sometimes, what people want and what they need are two different things. That's one of the underlying principles I want to share with you here. **It's all about serving.** That's where this whole "selling is serving" idea comes from. You're giving people what they want; you're serving them, and if you do that for enough people, you're going to get rich.

NUMBER 29: Keep giving your customers more of what they bought from you the first time. You've seen me say that before. It's all about variations on a theme. What do people want? More of what they bought from you the first time.

NUMBER 30: Find just a few people you can really trust, who are super-talented in the areas you're weak in, and do everything you can to keep those people on your team. Grab them tight, give them whatever they want, love them, take good care of them, don't let go of them. These people are the most important people in your life and your business.

NUMBER 31: Express yourself fully. Don't hold back. If there's one thing you can say about me with this book, it's that I've just tried to be myself. I haven't tried to show off. I'm not a professional speaker or writer. I am what I am. Too many people are playing games; they're trying to be perfect, they're trying to be too polished, and they're not being real — and everybody knows that. Whether you like me or not, at least you know I've been real with you. I've been sharing things from my heart; hopefully you'll at least respect me for that. I want you to do the same thing, when it comes to everything that you do in your life. Just be yourself and express yourself fully, and don't hold back. **It's the people in this world who really don't give a damn about what anybody else thinks of them that we end up respecting the most.** It's the people who are trying to be perfect and polished, who are trying to go through their whole lives pleasing everybody else, who end up getting no respect. I just want you to just take off all the filters; that's what I've tried to do with this book. Express yourself fully.

> The true art of selling is to make people feel that they are the ones chasing you!

NUMBER 32: Everything is difficult until it becomes easy. You've got to be willing and even eager to pay the biggest price possible for the things that you want the most. We always value what we pay the most for — and the skills that it takes to make millions of dollars, like product development, copywriting, good marketing skills, everything I've shared with you that has been responsible for the millions of dollars we've made, has come with a price. **You'll pay that price and you'll feel good about it. It *will* get easier, but you've got to be willing to pay the price and understand**

that there's a learning curve involved. I love what Ray Bradbury says: He says that to be a good writer is real simple. What you have to do is write 20,000 pages, and by the time you write those 20,000 pages, you'll have put in the time and work necessary for your writing to be where it needs to be. After you get past those 20,000 pages, you're a good writer. I love that quote, because it expresses what I've been trying to share with you. It's no accident that the greatest direct-response marketing copy writers, the ones who write sales letters that generate millions of dollars, are usually those who have been doing it for at least ten years, and quite possibly twenty years or more. **Experience is important; there's only one way you can get it, though. You've got to pay the price and get started today.**

NUMBER 33: Fall in love with the few things that make you the most money: product development, marketing, and copy writing. Fall in love with doing those things. They're challenging, fun, rewarding — and the more you love them, the more you're going to get lost in them; and the more your skills are going to develop along with your knowledge and experience. **You'll gain tremendous confidence.**

NUMBER 34: At any given time you've got to know what the five most important things are in your life. I've got a list right here in front of me; and it's my five things. I know what they all are, and when I read that list I can see if I am on target, if I'm moving in the right direction. **It helps you to stay focused.**

NUMBER 35: Stay hungry. Remember where you came from, where you are now, and where you want to go. Never lose that desire. I'm just going to assume that you're hungry. It's a good assumption on my part, I think, and I want you to keep that hunger. Sometimes you'll get the success that you've longed for, and you start coasting. You can't do it; stay hungry. That's where playing it as a game helps.

NUMBER 36: Get really good at a few things that make you the most money, then delegate everything else. That's related to Number 33. Just stay totally focused on just those few things that make you the most money. Let everything else go. Find other people you can work through who have skills that can help you fill in all the other gaps.

NUMBER 37: Direct response marketing is math and psychology; that's all. You've got to really understand people — that's the psychology — and then, with every promotion, you need to understand the money math. It's really easy to do.

NUMBER 38: Business is an accelerated lifestyle. You get more of the good and more of the bad. For me, it's been a major roller coaster ride. I've experienced so many wonderful things in business, and it's challenging; it really is. But it's also rewarding and exciting and depressing, and there are things that will break your heart. **There are problems and obstacles and difficulties, and it's the best of everything that life has to offer.** You get more of everything; you get more of the good, you get more of the bad. It's a wonderful way to live, but keep that in mind; it's an accelerated lifestyle. That will help you deal with some of the pressures you have to deal with.

NUMBER 39: Money and material things are great, but true confidence doesn't come from having things; it comes from handling things. I've got to say that to you one more time — I know you want to make money. **That was me, too; I wanted to become a multimillionaire, and that's all I cared about in the beginning. But money and material things...**

well, they're great. Enjoy them; they're your trophies, and the more you work hard for them, the more you can appreciate them. That's why it's good to pay the price you need to pay. You hear about people who win the lottery; their whole lives are destroyed, because they're not prepared for the

> **F**ind the buyers who can buy the most and you won't have to find the most buyers! Less is more!

wealth. But once you've paid the price for it, you'll really feel good about it. You'll know you deserve it because you worked your ass off for it. **But true confidence, and true happiness also, doesn't come from having things; it comes from your ability to handle things.** That's a good place to wrap this up, one related to the ninth concept I shared. That's the Jim Rohn quote that says, "Don't wish things were easier, wish that you were better."

A lot of people want to make a fortune because they're looking for a perfect life. They've got this image in their heads that they're going to make millions of dollars, and then they're just going to kick back on some sandy beach, somewhere exotic, and everything's going to be perfect. Well, I have my fantasies too, but at least I know that they're fantasies. I want *you* to know that they're fantasies, too. **Look, the greatest thing about business and reaching all of your goals is just what Jim Rohn suggested: it's who you become in the process. Life here is limited.** All of our lives, we don't know how much longer we have here. This could be your last day; you could have another decade; you could have another five decades. **It's who we become in life, through the process of working towards our goals, that's the most important thing,** and having confidence means that you're facing all the adversity that comes your way, all the challenges. **You're taking charge of your life, you're**

willing to do the things most people are unwilling to do.

You can make a lot of money, sure, and that's great. **But true confidence comes from your knowing, just that knowing, that you have the ability to handle anything that comes your way.** Fear is a real enemy of success, but if you knew you could handle anything and everything that comes your way, there would be no fear. I've dealt with a lot of fear and a lot of insecurities; I've had a lot of challenges in my life, and I've tried to share them with you in a very open and honest way.

The greatest feeling is *not* just having millions of dollars, it's knowing that you overcame all that crap that was in your way. You've developed some real skills and abilities, and you've tried to focus on serving people and helping people. **In order to get your money, you've tried to offer tremendous value to other people, and that's a great, great feeling, especially when those people will use your ideas, your help and support and guidance, to do big things with their lives.**

There's no better feeling.

CHAPTER

12

The End of Your Wealth-Making Journey

The subject of this last chapter is *The End of Your Wealth-Making Journey*. Think about that. By the time you're done with this chapter, **you're going to have a complete road map from here to success.**

It's always easier to find your way if you know where you're going from the very beginning. You may be new to this path; you may have been on this journey for a long time. If that's the case, it may be that you're confused, you're frustrated, and you don't always know exactly what to do. You have to learn all these new things just to get in the door; **there's a painful learning curve, and we all have to go through it.** I see it on the faces of my clients when I meet them in person at our seminars and workshops. Well, my colleagues and I have been there ourselves. We know how confusing some of this can get — which is why I'm hoping that at least some of what I'm going to discuss in this chapter will put an end to your confusion, and help you truly understand what you're trying to accomplish here. That's when you can stop focusing on today, and get an end strategy in place that will serve you well, far into the future.

Most people don't focus much on where they're going or where they're *trying* to get. They focus on today, and sometimes that's out of necessity. We're busier than ever before, so it's hard to get past today. We tend to run around in circles and do the same things repeatedly... and it tires us out, doesn't it? We're stuck in the same routine; we go through another day, and all of a sudden, we look back and we say, "How did we get here?" A year passes, then two; then it's five years; and ten, twenty, thirty years pass, and you really didn't get anywhere. You look back and have regrets, and wonder what happened. How did you get where are today without getting anything done?

Well, now that you've gotten started and there's some momentum there, this chapter's strategies are going to help you get over that hump, so you can take action and chart your course. **You'll be able to plan what you do today based on what your goals are and where you're trying to go tomorrow,** sort of like a pilot taking off in an airplane. If a pilot took off without planning his destination, he'd get up in the air and fly around aimlessly. Sure, he'd probably end up somewhere — but the somewhere wouldn't necessarily be where he wanted to go. A pilot *has* to chart his course in advance. He has to know exactly where he's going, and he has to point his airplane in the right direction to accomplish that. If he's got to fly from L.A. to Hawaii, he knows exactly how to get there. The cool thing is that during that flight, the plane is slightly off course well over 90% of the time due to wind currents, the jet stream, and other factors. But it's got the automatic computer system that guides it right back — so it constantly readjusts itself. The pilot and autopilot always know exactly where the end goal is.

Life is a lot like that. **You have to know where you're trying to get to in order to figure out what you need to do today and tomorrow, and on into next week, next month, and next year in order to get there.** This is something we don't focus on enough, and a lot of experts don't talk about it at all. They want to talk about what you need to do *today,* and so you get caught up in the today without any real clear objective in mind — and you end up flying around aimlessly.

One of my favorite quotes (and I'll paraphrase it slightly, because it's from the 1800s) says that a person can tolerate any situation if they just keep a strong enough goal in mind. **If there's hope for the future, there's strength for today.** If you've got a really great, powerful goal that's driving you, you don't always know exactly how you're going to figure out how to achieve it; sometimes you don't have a clue, but at least the goal is there. It's a road map, a destination, and if you keep it in mind, you can figure out how to reach that destination. **It's always easier to find your way if you know where you want to wind up.**

Next, let's look at with a series of questions to ask yourself before you start your journey. The idea is to help you define where you want to be, and what will make you happy. This will let you document your goals in writing, so you can focus on them and be motivated to stay the course. Until you know where you want to wind up, it's tough to write that down. **Let's start out with the definition of a destination, first of all.** I think this is a good thing to understand.

One thing I've learned during my years in DRM is that almost all of the profits in your business are going to

> **M**otivation is an internal thing. Nobody can give it to you. *You must keep looking for reasons to win!*

come from the back end. When I was first getting started in marketing, I didn't understand what the end of my journey would be. Nowadays the end of my journey is very clear, and it's connected with the fact that mostly, **the goal for my business is to make profits — just like everybody's goal for their business should be.** That's one of the end results. The 80/20 rule means that you need to spend more of your time and effort doing more business with your existing customers. **A good 80% of your profits are going to come from that back-end business, with no more that 20% being generated on the front end.** This information allows you to get more specific, and to define where you want to go in your journey.

For example, my friend and colleague Eric Bechtold's ultimate goal is have ten thousand individuals working directly with him, buying from him in a vacuum. What he means is that he wants their undivided attention, so when he puts something in front of them, they respond right away. He's not competing with a bunch of other people; they're focused on him and his sales materials. Ten thousand is specific number that Eric set as a goal. He figures if he can get to that point — and you always want to set your goals high — his journey will be accomplished. **At that point, he can pretty much print money on demand, if you will, by coming up with a new offer and plugging it into his mailing list.** At the moment, he's about a quarter of the way there.

I wanted to provide that example right away, so that you would understand the types of specific **cause-and-effect scenarios** involved here. You start out on your journey with nobody even knowing who you are. As you roll out your marketing pieces and get out there in the marketplace, people start to understand who you are, and they start to realize that you're a good person to do business with. You put your offers out there, and eventually you've got some brand equity, where people are paying attention to you. **Eventually, you get to the point where you've got people who are buying everything you put out there.** What you're selling is an integral part of the part of the ongoing relationship you have with your customers.

At M.O.R.E., Inc., **we know exactly how much money we want to bring in every single month; that's our destination, at least on a monthly basis.** I've got that number written down in several places around my house, and I'm always thinking about it. **I live with that number always.** When we don't hit it, I feel it deeply — and it makes me frustrated. I think frustration is a good thing. It doesn't *feel* good, but it's good anyway as long as you're frustrated for the right reasons. **When we're not hitting those numbers that we have to have every single month, I'm spurred to do things better, to tighten things up, to try new things.** Our goal is very real; we have specific things we put into action, processes we put into place to help us achieve that goal, and we're extremely disappointed when we miss it. We analyze our numbers daily, weekly, and of course monthly, and we know at the beginning of the month — after just a couple of days — whether we're on or off target. Are we where we need to be, or are we a little low? Are we a little high? Where are we at? We do this because we want to know where we'll be at the end of every month. **And by the way, that monthly goal also translates into an annual goal; and of course we know on a monthly basis how we're doing over the course of a year.**

The important thing is to have a goal, to have your end in mind. I encourage you to be specific with it, because too many people have generic, broad goals — and there's no penalty in their mind if they don't hit those goals. If your goal is just to make millions of dollars, that's probably not that good a goal for you. **A better one might be to take a million dollars a year and divide it out so you know how much money you need to make every day, every week, and every month.**

We're always looking at those numbers, because that's where it starts with us. **The strategies all evolve out of the numbers.** We determine first how much money we want to make every month; and I won't give that figure here, but it's very high, definitely in the seven figures. Then from that point forward, Chris Lakey and I develop specific marketing strategies to get us where we want to go. The strategies become a little clearer when you start that way. We know the size of our average package; we know how big our market is. That tells us how many packages we need to sell.

Obviously, the end means different things to different people. We work from a specific amount of money, while Eric Bechtold aims for a specific number of customers. Maybe your end goal is

> **T**est everything! Sometimes it takes a lot of wrong answers to get to the right ones.

making enough money, consistently enough, that you can quit your job. Whatever the case, **when you're off that goal, you need to immediately figure out why so you can get back on point.** That's why you need to start with very specific goals — because **you'll never make the abstract ones.** They're not specific enough, and they're easily avoidable. It's easy to say, "I want to make millions of dollars!" and then, when it doesn't happen, to just pass it off. But if you sincerely have a goal to make, say, $100,000 a week, then if you don't, you know you've missed your goal and you have to adjust your game plan. If your goal is to make $1,000 a week, you can get there. You know how many products you need to sell to reach that goal. You know how many sales letters you need to send, how many ads you need to place.

It all starts with that end in mind, followed by formulating your plan to get there. Sticking to the plan is important, because you can't just have a goal and then randomly go through your week, month, or year and then look back and wonder why you didn't hit it. **You've got to constantly be aiming at that target, and making constant little adjustments** like an airplane does with its course. You've got to adjust every day, every week, every month so that you can hit your goal. Maybe $1,000 seems like a good amount to you... but if your goal is $5,000 a week, then if you make just $1,000 you know you've come up really short. But if you *don't* have the $5,000 weekly goal, then maybe $1,000 a week may seem like enough, and you accept it. **Do that, and you're limiting yourself.**

The times in my life when I've made the most money were when I've had those firm goals in place — and the times when I've suffered financially have been the times when I took my eyes off of the prize. I quit focusing on my goals; and as they say, **wherever your focus goes, that's where your power goes. What you focus on really does expand.** If you don't have some firm goal in mind, whether it's a dollar amount, number of customers, or both, then you're causing yourself a lot of unnecessary misery. Just saying "I want to get rich" is not a goal. **There's a formula to getting rich, and that formula is very simple: get a large enough group of people to consistently give you money, at a large enough profit margin per transaction.** This is the kind of thing you need to start wrapping your mind around. How many customers do you need? How much profit do you need to make per sale in order to make your goal? When you do come up with a number, and then write that down; it makes a big difference.

Here are a few questions I'd like you to ask yourself. **First**

of all, can you define your destination — do you know where you want to go? **Next, what will make you happy?** What will satisfy your desires when you get there? You need to think deeply on these subjects — because again, there's no point in running around like a maniac trying to achieve a nebulous goal. **Identifying your goals and internalizing them, making them a part of you so that you feel pain if you don't achieve them, will motivate you.** That's why I keep that specific monthly dollar goal posted all over my house. I can't walk around without that goal staring me in the face. That's good, because it's constantly readjusting me; instead of getting lazy one night and saying, "Okay, tonight I'm just gonna kick my feet up with a bowl of popcorn and veg out for a couple of hours," I might decide to work on a sales letter to help get that goal up to where we need to be. That way, I can experience some bliss and some joy when we attain those goals.

And that's another reason for defining them — so that you can celebrate when you achieve your goals. And once you've celebrated, what do you do? **You set more lofty goals!** You get to the point where you say, "Wow, I was able to achieve that — now what am I capable of doing? Let's set even higher goals." It's kind of like a path to success. **You take each little stone at a time; each goal gets you from one place to another, and if you keep that mentality, you'll be surprised how far it's going to take you.**

Another thing I wanted to point out here is that in addition to thinking about your own goals, you have to realize that you don't get to your destination without also thinking about the destinations of others. This is also a very important thing to think about. **The end of your journey is not going to be accomplished without you wrapping your mind around**

what's going on in other people's minds to motivate them.
There's the psychology factor again. The reality here is that if
you want to get rich, if you want people to part with their money,
if you want to make a sale, you have to understand what's in
their heads. **That's what selling is: giving people something of
value so that they'll part with their
hard-earned cash.** Well, if you want to
do that, not only do you have to have
your own goals in mind, you must be
mindful of other people's goals.

> Spend <u>more</u> money to attract the <u>smaller</u> group of *the prime prospects* you most want as long-term customers.

It's kind of like when you take
your hands and interlace your fingers;
**your personal marketing journey is very interlaced with your
customer base.** If you want to make money you also have to get
to know your customer; again, you have to figure out what their
goals are, their desires, their pains, and frustrations. What can
you provide them to help them along in their journey so that they
can help you along in yours? As Zig Ziglar taught us, **you can
get whatever you want, as long as help enough people get
what *they* want.** That's something you really need to understand.

So like an airline or ship with its charts, start plotting a way
to get from point A to point B. Once you've got your goal in
mind, you can sit down and really start pushing towards that goal.
The best way to begin that journey is to first decide, "Okay, who
am I going to be working with? Who is excited enough out there?
Who's got pain and frustration that I can help with?" **One of the
key strategies to DRM is to find a frustrated group of
individuals and sell to their pain; that's a particularly good
motivator.** Most of the best markets out there are like that; the
diet industry, for example, where people are frustrated with their
weight. It's depressing them. They're jealous of looking out and

seeing all these skinny people. They want that, too, so they're angry and they're frustrated. That's why the diet industry is a booming industry. So is the home-based business industry. People are frustrated, because they're part of the rat race and they're not making enough money. They're sick of banging their heads on their desk for eight hours and counting down the seconds until when they can leave every single day, so they're looking for a way out. **There's a reason we're tightly focused on business opportunities, because it's a very good marketplace.**

The point is, both your journey and the journey of the people you're working with are very closely related, so you have to keep your mind focused on both in order to achieve your own goals. If you're focused just on what you want, you won't be focused on what your customers want — and ultimately, it all starts with the market. People tend to put the greatest emphasis on the products and services, **but the market is the most important factor in the business equation.** Think like McDonald's or Starbucks. McDonald's used to be just a burger and fry place — but recently they've become this place where you can get healthy food, too, because the people in their marketplace want healthier choices. As for Starbucks, for years it's been known as the place to buy expensive coffee. More recently, they're seeing a lot of competition in the coffee market. So what's Starbucks doing? They now have a $1 cup of plain black coffee, like everyone else. They've adapted to the marketplace in order to try to keep giving customers what they want.

There are endless examples of businesses using this principle to their advantage. They've got their goals; they've got their financial targets they want to reach. But they've got targets that they see through their customers' eyes as well, and so they're trying to give their customers what their customers want.

If you can find someone's biggest wants and deliver them, then your own biggest wants will follow. You've got to look at your goals through the prism of your customers and *their* goals.

Ultimately, the products and services you want to sell will evolve and revolve around the market that you're serving. **Every great fortune that's ever been earned in the past, and will ever be earned in the future, is built on creating solutions that solve problems.** That's what we're all in business to do, which we accomplish by giving people what they want the most. **And let me re-emphasize the fact that what they generally want is an end to a certain pain they have, whether that be emotional or physical.** In our case it's emotional. People hate their jobs, they want financial security, and they're worried about the future. They don't trust Social Security to be around when they retire. And even if they think it *will* be around, they know it's never going to be enough. **Plus, people want a business opportunity because they want something to hope for and to dream about.** That's part of what makes life special. People need hope, and that's another great thing we do: we're giving people things they can get excited about. Our opportunities let them move forward and keep active... and of course, it's fun to make money.

Part of the way that you begin with the end in mind is to find companies to emulate, companies that are doing things like you want to do, that are already serving the markets you want to serve. **Look at the business opportunity market.** There are many, many different companies out there, some of them doing some amazing things, and the market has really evolved over the years. We've seen an astonishing amount of change in our market since 1988, and you'd better believe we keep a very close eye on what other people are doing. **We don't copy them — we try to find ways to beat them, to do things even better, with**

our own unique twist.

And we actually like competition. It really amazes me how some people think competition is a bad thing. I love competition; bring it on, baby! **I want competition because I want to try to be better.** I want to try to step up my game and improve upon it. Without competition, the business wouldn't be nearly as fun. When you've got competitors, you look closely at other companies to find out what they're doing. **You get on their mailing lists and buy stuff from them.** You don't do it through the eyes of a consumer; you get on the other side of the cash register, and you think about it from the stance of a business person. **You start looking for themes and patterns, to get a clearer idea of what you want to do.**

I've already talked about setting goals as a way to start developing that clear idea of where you want to go, and that's a good start. It's like going to the gym: something you have to do on a regular basis to get better. **You work at it every day;** you look for models, you examine what people both inside and outside of your industry are doing right, and you try to piece it all together with your own style, so you're not just some copycat. Copycats never really last long-term. Oftentimes they'll get

> People re-buy the most by selling them the same way you sold them before.

started, make money initially, and then crash for lack of initiative and inventiveness. **Until you learn how to blend all your own ideas with what other people are doing, you're never going to make money long-term.** You have to bring to the table as much as you can of your own ideas, creativity, spirit, and talent, and eventually, experience.

So far, I've discussed how to figure out what makes your

market tick. You define your market, if you haven't done that yet; do you want to sell to the business opportunity market, to chiropractors, to dentists? Then look for their sources of frustration and pain (whether emotional or physical) and create solutions that address those points. **Immerse yourself in that market so that you can identify those sore spots.** What can you provide to ease that pain or frustration? What can you bring to the table?

This is how you define your front-end offer, the tool you're going to use to capture the minds of your consumers, to get them engaged in purchasing products from you and to get them in your customer database. Think of it, if you will, as a mousetrap — and I don't mean that in a demeaning way. **The goal is to capture your audience base, to pull them in so you can help them.** Once you find an attractive piece of bait, just continue to use it until it stops effectively trapping people.

I like the mousetrap analogy because, first of all, you have to think with the end in mind. Then you have to define your audience base. *Then* you have to come up with the bait — what are you going to do in order to get involved in this game? You can't stand on the sidelines and make all sorts of grandiose gestures and set empty goals and never really get in the game. This is where you start implementing. The key idea here is that once you have people coming in to your sales funnel, they start buying things from you. **And remember, how much pain and frustration exists in your marketplace will determine how long these people are going to need you.** If there's a lot of pain and frustration, buying one little widget from you probably isn't going to satisfy that. But if they continue to see you as the answer, they also continue to see you as somebody they can come back to, again and again. Remember that little three-step process. **Finding a group of individuals, then getting them to**

make purchases from you, at a high enough profit margin, over and over again, will make you rich.

What you also need to realize is that we're in the business of buying sales at a discount. **We want to bring people in, and then have other things that we can sell to them once we have them.** And we want to make sure that we're making our numbers, as I outlined earlier. That subject dovetails nicely into this one. You want to be looking at your numbers regularly and saying, "Okay, I'm spending this amount of money. How much am I making? Am I on target? Are we going to hit these numbers?" Now, of course you're going to start with relatively small numbers. You don't want to start out by trying to hit a seven-figure month, like we do at M.O.R.E., Inc., these days. We've been in the business for a long time, and yes, that may be a place you get to in the future. **But for now, you need to start modestly — yet still aggressively.** If you think you might be happy making $1,000 a month, or $1,000 a week, jack that up to $5,000 or $10,000.

Here's an example of that. I remember when my friend and colleague Eric Bechtold first came to me, when he was just getting out of an ad agency and his goals were way, way, low compared to what was possible. When he told me his goal, I said to him, "Well, that's a good goal — but trust me, you'll be able to do that easily, plus a lot more." And I was right! Eric pulls in so much money now that we call him "Young King Midas." I knew how much money he wanted to make, but I also knew how smart and ambitious he was — and I knew the potential of the marketplace, and how many millions of dollars were to be made, because I'd already generated millions of dollars on my own.

You know, if you tell the average person who's never made

any substantial money in their life that you're going to make millions of dollars someday, they're going to either think you're crazy or they're going to laugh at you. Some will try to belittle you. But if you go to somebody who started from scratch and has already made millions, they're likely to support you. They may well do whatever they can to help you, because in business we all work together — or at least we do in our

> **When you find your successful formula — don't change it! ...At least until the numbers start going downhill.**

market. That's one of the things I just love about direct response in general. **It's fun to be able to befriend your competitors and do business with them.** Everybody makes more money, and your friendships are built around your businesses because your businesses are important to you.

And even if you just want to beat the competition, it's not that hard to differentiate yourself. One specific way to do this is something called the **unique selling position, or USP.** That's what different about your company that separates it from everyone else. It took us a long time to figure that out, and it took us even longer develop it properly — and we're still kind of developing it after 21 years. The market does change, and you continually have to find ways to improve.

Part of the reason people in this business get so frustrated is that not only do they not have a clear end in mind at first, sometimes when they do start getting that clear idea of where they want to end up at, they become even more frustrated. Now they start to realize, "Holy crap! Look at all the stuff I have to do!" **But rest assured, all these things are the kinds of things where you can earn while you learn.** You don't have to figure it out overnight; and in fact, you'll never figure it all out. It's a game, and the game keeps changing. And besides, success is a moving target — so you constantly have to adjust your aim. The market never stops changing, and you know what? That's a good thing. **That should excite you, because as long as it's a rabid, every-changing market, all those changes spell profits.** The more you're willing to bend and flex with it, the more you'll be able to stay on top of things and cash in on whatever's hot — and there's always something hot. That's part of the joy for me, because there's always something new and exciting. The idea here is that when you start thinking about these things seriously, and you start realizing what's really possible, the whole world opens up to you.

Another question to think about at this point is this: Why should your customer continue to do business with you? **What can you provide on that back end for your customers that will make them stick with you, once they've taken your cheese?** Remember, Eric's goal is to get 10,000 people buying in a vacuum from him. That means they're not only in his trap, but they're happy to be there — because they understand that any time Eric offers them something, it's something good for them, and they want it right away. So ideally, they'll continue to buy.

Hopefully, these questions and concepts are starting to focus your mind on how to take those goals in hand and set out on the journey toward your destination. You plot a course, and figure out what pieces need to be where in order to effectively move you from point A to point B. We talk about the money a lot, and of course the money is important; but remember, the theme of this chapter is "the end of your wealth-making journey." **The real joy has always been the journey; it's never just the destination.** The fact is, sometimes when you reach your goals, they turn out to be anticlimactic. It's like that old Patsy Cline song that says, "Is this all there is?" Once you find that destination, then, you've got to set bigger goals or different goals, and start on a *new* journey. **You always want to be moving forward.** You need a destination just to keep you focused on your journey, to be sure you're not wasting a lot of time. **Get in the game. Enjoy the journey. Have fun.**

Because the truth is, this game of making money *is* fun. It's thrilling; it's like a hunt. When I was a kid, we used to go hunting all the time; and the fun was just in doing the hunting, it wasn't necessarily the killing part. In fact, that's why I quit hunting, because I didn't like to kill — but I always liked to hunt. That's why people go fishing, that's why they go hunting, that's why they go on all kinds of adventures. That's why they take trips down roaring rivers or up to the tops of high mountains.

The worst thing you could do is stagnate, or find yourself facing a stagnant marketplace where there's not a lot of new things happening, not a lot of change. **Part of the fun is the change, and the turnover, and the cycles that businesses go through.** It's very difficult to innovate in an old business or an old marketplace, where things are always done the same way, and the customers expect the same things over and over and buy the same thing over and over, because they're conditioned to act a certain way and to do certain things. That's a difficult place to make money in.

But if you're in a marketplace where there are new trends and shifts in emphasis, or even paradigms, **you can profit from those shifts.** You can ride those waves of success, as long as you're always alert and watching for the next wave, the next trend, the next shift in the marketplace. Since the market is constantly changing, your goals, that end target, have to move to some degree as well. And it's usually a short-term target. In this marketplace, especially in this part of our history, there's so much happening with technology, in the way we do business online and offline. **Just the process of doing business changes so much that you have to constantly be adjusting your strategies and setting new goals.** Take that monthly goal I talked about earlier; that's just for right now. A year or two from now, that goal might be different. I can't see it being any lower, but maybe it'll be a little higher. And maybe we'll have

> **A** half-baked idea well executed is much better than that "perfect" idea that is <u>always</u> just around the corner!

shifted the way we're going about trying to reach that goal. That's because we know that if you're in tune with the fact that things change, you can be in position to benefit from those changes by being nimble, responsive, and innovative — and have a great time doing it.

Even if a marketplace seems a little staid, you might be able to find the excitement if you just do a little digging. We've got a husband-and-wife team who are part of our Direct Response Network; they're out of San Diego, and they're in a business that's anything but exciting to me. It sounds like the most boring business in the world, but as of two years ago they'd done $50 million worth of business in the previous seven years. They're clearing huge sums of money selling, of all things, nuts and bolts. Honestly, they sell nuts and bolts — and doing so excites them. The reason they're excited about their business is because of the lifestyle that it has afforded them. That's really what gets them out of bed in the morning. They built their company together, and they sell through a worldwide market. I can't imagine a more boring business — but whatever turns your crank, go for it.

This is what I want you to pull out of this whole discussion. **Keeping your goals in mind and understanding where you want to go is just a way to get engaged in the process and to manifest your reality.** Because what you focus on becomes your reality; if you keep thinking about it and keep moving toward it, taking little baby steps every day, eventually you'll wind up there. **Remember, marketing is a three-step process. NUMBER ONE is attracting qualified leads. NUMBER TWO is converting the highest percentage possible into sales. NUMBER THREE is reselling the largest possible number of these customers.** And that's it; only three steps. That's what you need to understand about the marketing side of it.

Once you have the answers to the questions that I've presented here, you're going to know who you are, where you want to be, who your audience is, what you're going to offer them in order to get there. **Once you know all that, it's just a matter of figuring out what your mousetrap's going to be, and figuring out a way to put it where there's likely to be a mouse.** You might start by running a small little classified ad, or just sending out a few hundred postcards. And that's another thing I'd like to leave you with. Figuring out your destination is one thing, but when you're figuring out the steps that you're going to take to get there — when you come up with ideas and put them into motion — **make sure that you test things in a small way first.** Once you find something that's working, then roll it out big. That'll keep you out of trouble. If you find you're going the wrong direction, those baby steps let you replot and adjust your course a little. You're not going to get into a financial situation where you can't readjust. **You never want to throw all your eggs in one basket;** you want to feel your way along, if you will. Eventually you'll get to the point where you can stride forward in confidence, really roll out big, and get to that first destination you've set before you — so you can pause, take a deep breath, and plan for that next destination.

Starting with your end in mind is the only way to start, because otherwise, how do you ever know if you've accomplished anything? So many small business owners — and I'm talking about a huge percentage — have no destination in mind at all. Every day is the same day lived over and over. They're working hard, they're putting in a lot of hours, and yet they're not making enough money. But when you sit down with them and say, "Hey, look, what's your marketing plan? Tell me, I want to see it, I want to help you here," you discover that they don't have one. And if you ask them what their goals are, they really don't have any — or if they do, it's something like "Pay the bills." Or they've got a far off fantasy that someday they're going to sell their business and retire.

The two men that I've loved most in my life, my father and my stepfather, both did a terrible job planning their futures. They were great men, I loved both of them dearly, and I think about them all the time. For the last 20 years of his life, my stepdad was in business. And I tried to help him; I tried to give him some ideas, but he just was so much against them that I might as well not have tried. At first, I thought it was just him, because he was one of the most stubborn people I've known. But over the last 15-20 years, I've run into so many business owners who are exactly like my stepdad. To them, it's not a business; it's just a job. They just go to work every day, and it's not exciting.

To me, **business is an exciting game; it's something you play to win.** Show me any game where you can't keep score, and I'll show you the most boring game on the planet. That may be fine when you're a kid and you're trying to have fun, but when you're older, **you've got to be able to keep score;** otherwise, what's the point? You play to win; and winning isn't the "only thing," by the way, Vince Lombardi notwithstanding. **It's the desire to win that's the only thing.** Because as I've said, many of your goals will seem anticlimactic once you hit them. So you've got a goal to make a million dollars? Well, once you make a million, you'll say, "Hey, wait a minute, I thought this was going to make my life a million times better." Your life probably *is* better, but not by as much as you thought. The real fun is in playing the game. **It's the sport, it's the hunt, it's the chase; it's the thrill of all of that.**

Keep hunting for your next big idea. **You never know when or where you'll find it.**

And that's what I hope that you'll learn along the way: **that the journey is the reward. That said, you still have to know where you want to wind up, or you're never going to get there...** and it's no fun being lost. I see so many businesspeople who dream of owning their own businesses but live nothing but a nightmare, because every day they're doing the best they know how to, but they're getting nowhere. They're not focused on hitting any kind of a goal. They're not going for it, because they don't even know what they're going for. They're locked into survival; that's all. They're just trying to survive... and if that's your goal, you don't have a goal. That's just existence. **Real success is grabbing for something outside of your current reach.** It's something to get excited about for the future. It's something that moves you forward, not just going through the same motions that you went through yesterday and the day before. If you're just getting by, if your goal is just to survive in business, then you probably shouldn't be in business. There are a lot of good jobs to be had out there; and if that's your way of looking at the world, that may be a better route for you.

If you're serious about your goals, then I'd encourage you to write them down and think about them. Put them in a place where you can see them every day, so you can be held to that standard. Share those goals with other people who can hold you accountable, so that they can ask you, "Hey, did you mail out 1,000 letters today? Because you said you needed to mail out 1,000 letters today to reach your goal. I'm just checking up on you to see if you really did drop those in the mail." Or "Did you place that ad today?" or "How many sales did you bring in today? Okay, you didn't reach your goal, so tomorrow you've got to bring in an extra "X" number of sales to make up for it." **Go find some people that can hold you to that standard;** and incidentally, don't just get a family member who might ask you for a day or two and then let you go. A fellow businessman or a friend might be a better choice.

And remember that goals can be adjusted, so don't be too hard on yourself if you don't make them. Be disappointed, sure; as I mentioned at the beginning of the chapter, we're upset when we don't make our goals, but it's not the end of the world. We adjust our goals and we keep going at it. **The worst thing you can do is give up and feel defeated.** Goals can be modified as you chart your course, and as you make adjustments along the way. That way, you'll be able to hone them and to keep moving forward.

So that's the main thing: **be a doer, not a talker.** Get out there and be active in your business, doing everything you can to achieve those goals, to set bigger goals, and to accomplish more.

www.ingramcontent.com/pod-product-compliance
Lightning Source LLC
Chambersburg PA
CBHW020159200326
41521CB00005BA/188